MIRACLES

EDITING AND PRODUCTION TEAM:

James F. Couch, Jr., Lyman Coleman, Sharon Penington, Cathy Tardif,
Christopher Werner, Matthew Lockhart, Erika Tiepel, Richard Peace,
Andrew Sloan, Keith Madsen, Mary Chatfield, Scott Lee

NASHVILLE, TENNESSEE

Published by Serendipity House Publishers

Nashville, Tennessee

International Standard Book Number: 1-57494-315-4

ACKNOWLEDGMENTS

Scripture quotations are taken from the Holman Christian Standard Bible,
© Copyright 2000 by Holman Bible Publishers. Used by permission.

Nashville, Tennessee

1-800-525-9563

www.serendipityhouse.com

Table of Contents

CORE VALUES

Community: The purpose of this curriculum is to build community within the body of believers around Jesus Christ.

Group Process: To build community, the curriculum must be designed to take a group through a step-by-step process of sharing your story with one another.

Interactive Bible Study: To share your "story," the approach to Scripture in the curriculum needs to be open-ended and right brain—to "level the playing field" and encourage everyone to share.

Developmental Stages: To provide a healthy program throughout the four stages of the life cycle of a group, the curriculum needs to offer courses on three levels of commitment: (1) Beginner Level—low-level entry, high structure, to level the playing field; (2) Growth Level—deeper Bible study, flexible structure, to encourage group accountability; (3) Discipleship Level—in-depth Bible study, open structure, to move the group into high gear.

Target Audiences: To build community throughout the culture of the church, the curriculum needs to be flexible, adaptable and transferable into the structure of the average church.

Mission: To expand the kingdom of God one person at a time by filling the "empty chair." (We add an extra chair to each group session to remind us of our mission.)

introduction

Each healthy small group will move through various stages as it matures.

Multiply Stage: The group begins the multiplication process. Members pray about their involvement in new groups. The "new" groups begin the life cycle again with the Birth Stage.

Birth Stage: This is the time in which group members form relationships and begin to develop community. The group will spend more time in ice-breaker exercises, relational Bible study and covenant building.

Develop Stage: The inductive Bible study deepens while the group members discover and develop gifts and skills. The group explores ways to invite their neighbors and coworkers to group meetings.

Growth Stage: Here the group begins to care for one another as it learns to apply what they learn through Bible study, worship and prayer.

Subgrouping: If you have nine or more people at a meeting, Serendipity recommends you divide into subgroups of 3–6 for the Bible study. Ask one person to be the leader of each subgroup and to follow the directions for the Bible study. After 30 minutes, the Group Leader will call "time" and ask all subgroups to come together for the Caring Time.

Each group meeting should include all parts of the "three-part agenda."

Ice-Breaker: Fun, history-giving questions are designed to warm the group and to build understanding about the other group members. You can choose to use all of the Ice-Breaker questions, especially if there is a new group member that will need help in feeling comfortable with the group.

Bible Study: The heart of each meeting is the reading and examination of the Bible. The questions are open, discover questions that lead to further inquiry. Reference notes are provided to give everyone a "level playing field." The emphasis is on understanding what the Bible says and applying the truth to real life. The questions for each session build. There is always at least one "going deeper" question provided. You should always leave time for the last of the "questions for interaction." Should you choose, you can use the optional "going deeper" question to satisfy the desire for the challenging questions in groups that have been together for a while.

Caring Time: All study should point us to actions. Each session ends with prayer and direction in caring for the needs of the group members. You can choose between several questions. You should always pray for the "empty chair." Who do you know that could fill that void in your group?

Sharing Your Story: These sessions are designed for members to share a little of their personal lives each time. Through a number of special techniques, each member is encouraged to move from low risk, less personal sharing to higher risk responses. This helps develop the sense of community and facilitates caregiving.

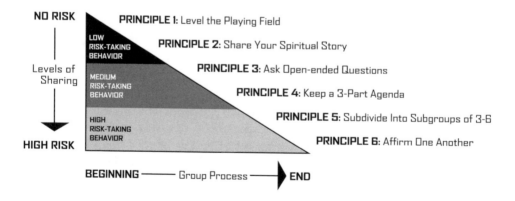

NO RISK

LOW RISK-TAKING BEHAVIOR

Levels of Sharing

MEDIUM RISK-TAKING BEHAVIOR

HIGH RISK-TAKING BEHAVIOR

HIGH RISK

PRINCIPLE 1: Level the Playing Field

PRINCIPLE 2: Share Your Spiritual Story

PRINCIPLE 3: Ask Open-ended Questions

PRINCIPLE 4: Keep a 3-Part Agenda

PRINCIPLE 5: Subdivide Into Subgroups of 3-6

PRINCIPLE 6: Affirm One Another

BEGINNING ——— Group Process ——▶ END

Group Covenant: A group covenant is a "contract" that spells out your expectations and the ground rules for your group. It's very important that your group discuss these issues–preferably as part of the first session.

GROUND RULES:

• Priority: While you are in the group, you give the group meeting priority.

• Participation: Everyone participates and no one dominates.

• Respect: Everyone is given the right to their own opinion and all questions are encouraged and respected.

• Confidentiality: Anything that is said in the meeting is never repeated outside the meeting.

• Empty Chair: The group stays open to new people at every meeting.

• Support: Permission is given to call upon each other in time of need–even in the middle of the night.

• Advice Giving: Unsolicited advice is not allowed.

• Mission: We agree to do everything in our power to start a new group as our mission.

GOALS:

• The time and place this group is going to meet is_____.

• Refreshments are _____ responsibility.

• Child care is _____ responsibility.

SESSION 1 : WATER INTO WINE

SCRIPTURE JOHN 2:1–11

WELCOME

Welcome to this study of Jesus' miracles. Together we will look at the miracles that Jesus performed and consider who Christ is and what powers we are given as we serve him.

What is the importance of these things we call miracles? Some see them as a validation of the authority of one sent by God. Thus, Moses was given the ability to perform certain miraculous acts to prove to the Israelites that he had indeed been sent by God. Jesus' miracles were seen as signs that he was not just an ordinary teacher. Nicodemus voiced this perspective when he said, "Rabbi, we know that you have come from God as a teacher, for no one could perform these signs You do unless God were with him" (3:2). Still, at least in Jesus' case, it seems that the miracles he did were more than ways of authenticating his work. First of all, not all people interpreted these miraculous events in the same way. Some people saw Jesus' miracles as acts of Satan, intended to deceive people (Matt. 12:22–28). Jesus also refused the Pharisees' request for a sign to authenticate his authority (Mark 8:11–12). He also refused to show a miracle to Herod, even though such an act may have influenced Herod to act on his behalf (Luke 23:8). If Jesus had been doing miracles just to prove who he was, such refusals would seem strange.

What other purpose would there be to performing miracles? It is far more in accord with the nature of Jesus' miracles to see them as an essential part of his message. Jesus' message would not be the same apart from the miracles, for they are the physical demonstrations of the news he announced regarding the kingdom of God. Without the miracles, Jesus would simply have been another prophet looking ahead to the coming of the kingdom. The healing of the blind, the lame, the leprous and the deaf; the raising of the dead; the verbal proclamation of the Good News of God's kingdom (Matt. 11:4–5)–all point together to the truth that in Jesus the kingdom of God has begun to break in upon the world.

Down through history, what people of spiritual perception have consistently learned is that the moment we put a limitation on God, God breaks through it! What we need to believe and understand is that God is a God who acts in this world, both through nature and over and above what is considered to be natural. As we look at the miracles of Jesus in this study, we will see that such a God of power is worthy of our greatest reverence and devotion.

ICE-BREAKER : CONNECT WITH YOUR GROUP | 15 MINUTES

LEADER: Be sure to read the introductory material in the front of this book prior to the first session. To help your group members get acquainted, have each person introduce him or herself and then take turns answering one or two of the Ice-Breaker questions. If time allows, you may want to discuss all three questions.

One thing we don't always understand is that Jesus appreciated many of the things we appreciate in life—including parties. He did not relegate himself to the sidelines of life, nor did he limit his activities to "religious" gatherings. But what he did was to bring the spirit of God to all of life. What has been your own history at parties? Share something about yourself by answering the following questions.

1. What was the biggest party you remember attending when you were a teenager? Was there something in particular you were celebrating? What made a party fun for you at that time? What made you uncomfortable?

2. What is the funniest thing that has happened to you at a wedding or wedding reception?

3. If you went to a party, and things were not going well, would you tend to step in and help, or would you sit back and leave it to others?

BIBLE STUDY : READ SCRIPTURE AND DISCUSS | 30 MINUTES

LEADER: Select a member of the group ahead of time to read aloud the Scripture passage. Then discuss the Questions for Interaction, dividing into subgroups of three to six. Be sure to save time at the end for the Caring Time.

Many of Jesus' miracles had a life-or-death impact—healing the lame, raising the dead, providing food for the hungry. But his miracles started with one that at first glance does not seem to have had the urgency of the others—he turned water into wine at a wedding celebration! And yet in that act also, Jesus showed that nothing is impossible with God, and that through the abundance of what God gives, there is always enough to go around. Read John 2:1-11, and note how the disciples react to this miracle.

Jesus Changes Water to Wine

2 On the third day a wedding took place in Cana of Galilee. Jesus' mother was there, and ²Jesus and His disciples were invited to the wedding as well. ³When the wine ran out, Jesus' mother told Him, "They don't have any wine."

⁴"What has this concern of yours to do with Me, woman?" Jesus asked. "My hour has not yet come."

⁵"Do whatever He tells you," His mother told the servants.

⁶Now six stone water jars had been set there for Jewish purification. Each contained 20 or 30 gallons.

⁷"Fill the jars with water," Jesus told them. So they filled them to the brim. ⁸Then He said to them, "Now draw some out and take it to the chief servant." And they did.

⁹When the chief servant tasted the water (after it had become wine), he did not know where it came from—though the servants who had drawn the water knew. He called the groom ¹⁰and told him, "Everybody sets out the fine wine first, then, after people have drunk freely, the inferior. But you have kept the fine wine until now."

¹¹Jesus performed this first sign in Cana of Galilee. He displayed His glory, and His disciples believed in Him.

John 2:1–11

QUESTIONS FOR INTERACTION

LEADER: Refer to the Summary and Study Notes at the end of this section as needed. If 30 minutes is not enough time to answer all of the questions in this section, conclude the Bible Study by answering questions 6 and 7.

1. Had your own mother been there at the wedding, how would her reactions have compared to what Jesus' mother did?

2. How do you imagine Jesus felt about his mother's suggestion that he do something about the wine running out?
   - ☐ Amused.
   - ☐ Interested in what she had to say.
   - ☐ Listening for the Father's direction.
   - ☐ Pleased at her concern.
   - ☐ Not eager to face the clamor that would follow such a miracle.
   - ☐ Other _____.

3. What do you learn of Jesus and Mary from the interchange in verses 3–5? What is the meaning of his response to her?

4. What is meant by the word "sign" (v. 11) to describe this miracle? What effect did this incident have on Jesus' new disciples?

5. While the master of the banquet was simply glad that the party was not spoiled, what might John want to show about Jesus' glory by using this as the first miracle in his gospel?

6. What is the "wine" level (zest for living) in your life at the moment?
    - ❐ Full.
    - ❐ Half-full.
    - ❐ Nearly running out.
    - ❐ Totally drained.
    - ❐ Miraculously renewed.

7. What area of your life needs to be rejuvenated if you are to truly celebrate life?
    - ❐ My belief in people.
    - ❐ My belief in myself.
    - ❐ My ability to trust God.
    - ❐ A childlike spirit.
    - ❐ A confidence in the future.
    - ❐ My finances—my ability to pay for the party!
    - ❐ Other _____.

GOING DEEPER:

If your group has time and/or wants a challenge, go on to this question.

8. The water that was changed into wine was actually contained in jars used for ceremonial cleansing (see note on v. 6). What is the significance of this?

CARING TIME : APPLY THE LESSON AND PRAY FOR ONE ANOTHER | 15 MIN.

LEADER: Take some extra time in this first session to go over the introductory material at the front of this book. At the close, pass around your books and have every-one sign the Group Directory, also found in the front of this book.

This is a very important time to develop your concern for each other and to express it by praying for one another.

1. Agree on the group covenant and ground rules that are described in the introduction to this book.

2. How can this group pray for you in relation to the "shortages" you reported in questions 6 and 7?

3. Share any other prayer requests and praises, and then close in prayer. Pray specifically for God to bring someone into your life next week to fill the empty chair.

Today we looked at Jesus' first miracle—the changing of water into wine at a wedding. We were reminded that Jesus loves to celebrate with us and provide us with everything we need. In the coming week, take some extra time to tell Jesus what you need to fill the shortages in your life, especially the one you mentioned in question 7. Next week we will consider the story of Jesus driving out an evil spirit, and the need to remove the evil from our own lives.

NOTES ON JOHN 2:1–11

Summary: This incident is the first of seven signs around which chapters 2–12 of John's gospel was built. These miracles (2:1–11; 4:43–54; 5:1–15; 6:1–13; 6:16–21; 9:1–11; 11:38–44) are specifically called "signs" because they are not simply acts of power, but are meant to demonstrate the glory of God in Jesus (1:14). They are presented so that the reader might share in the confession that "these are written so that you may believe Jesus is the Messiah, the Son of God, and by believing you may have life in His name" (20:31). In this story, the growing recognition of who Jesus is climaxes with the affirmation of the disciples' faith (v. 11).

2:1 wedding. Weddings were important social events for the community: a time when all the relatives and townspeople would gather to celebrate, often for up to a week. **Cana.** The exact location of this village (mentioned only here and in 4:46) is unknown, but it is believed to have been near Nazareth.

2:3 the wine ran out. This was potentially a very humiliating social situation. It would reflect badly on the host as someone too miserly to provide adequate refreshments for the guests. It would be seen as a sign that the guests were not really welcome. **They don't have any wine.** Why Jesus' mother approached Jesus with this concern is unknown, since there is nothing in the record that indicates he had done anything to make her expect he could solve the problem. It implies her awareness of his miraculous power.

2:4 woman. Other translations say "Dear woman." Jesus uses the same term to address other women (Matt. 15:28; Luke 13:12). It is not a harsh term, but it is an unusual term for a son to use with his mother. It might indicate he is preparing her for the time when she will not be relating to him as a mother would a child, but relating to him as her Lord. **My hour has not yet come.** John frequently uses phrases and words with double meanings. Here, this phrase appears to mean simply that it is not yet appropriate for him to act. However, the "time" or "hour" of Jesus has a theological meaning as well (7:6,8,30; 8:20; 12:23,27; 13:1). It is used to refer to those moments when Jesus reveals his majesty and authority, a process that culminates in his crucifixion (16:32; 17:1).

2:6 six stone water jars. Although not required by the Law, by Jesus' day many Jews, in order to show their devotion to God, practiced purification rituals based on those required of the priests (Ex. 30:19–20; Mark 7:1–4). For instance, water would be poured over the hands of the guests prior to the meal. A large event like this wedding would require a great deal of water for such cleansing. **20 or 30 gallons.** The drinking of wine did not have the associations with alcoholism and alcohol abuse as it does so often today. The use of wine was a way of showing hospitality to guests, an expression of one's desire that others join in as celebrants at a happy occasion. Jesus' provision of such an ample amount of wine puts him in the place of a host, generously and graciously providing for his guests.

2:9 the chief servant. This appears to have been an honored guest at the wedding, serving in a role somewhat akin to that of a modern-day toastmaster. **he did not know where it came from.** This parallels the theme throughout John's gospel that the identity of Jesus is revealed only to those he chooses. Others see but do not comprehend. **He called the groom.** Weddings were typically held at the home of the groom or of his parents. The groom would be the one responsible for planning the wedding.

2:10 Everybody sets out the fine wine first. Typically, the best wine would be served when the guests would be most able to appreciate it. Later on, when they are less likely to notice, a cheaper quality of wine would be introduced. The quality of this wine was such that the master of the banquet thought the bridegroom had for some reason reversed the normal procedure.

2:11 first sign. Although the other Gospels typically refer to Jesus' miracles with a word that lays the stress on their being works of power, John prefers to call them signs. This encourages his readers not to see these actions simply as the acts of a wonder worker, but as pointers to God's presence in Jesus, recognized by those who receive him (1:12). Likewise, they are physical and material illustrations of the spiritual life Jesus came to bring (6:26–27; 9:1–5,39). **His glory.** While the chief servant, or master of the banquet, failed to discern by whom the wine came, the disciples saw the reality behind the sign. This was their first glimpse of the light of God's glory manifested in Jesus.

SESSION 2 : JESUS DRIVES OUT AN EVIL SPIRIT

SCRIPTURE MARK 1:21–28

LAST WEEK

Last week we looked at Jesus' first miracle—turning water into wine. We gave some thought to what it meant about our own shortages and how God meets those needs. This week we turn our attention to the world of evil, and a time when Jesus drove an evil spirit out of a man. We will look at what that meant, and what we need to do to overcome the evil forces in our lives.

| ICE-BREAKER : CONNECT WITH YOUR GROUP | 15 MINUTES |

LEADER: Begin the session with a word of prayer. Have your group members take turns sharing their responses to one, two or all three of the Ice-Breaker questions. Be sure that everyone gets a chance to participate.

We all respond in different ways to those in authority. Some of us gladly follow, while others question everything. Get to know each other better by sharing some of your thoughts and experiences with authority figures in your life.

1. Who was the best teacher you remember having in grade school? What made this teacher so special?

2. How do you most frequently relate to people in authority?
   - ☐ I'm the original "rebel without a cause."
   - ☐ I'm a rebel *with* a cause.
   - ☐ I'm my own authority.
   - ☐ I show respect to authorities who earn it.
   - ☐ I do what I'm told.
   - ☐ Other _____.

3. What kind of person are you most likely to respect as a person of authority?
   - ☐ The "It's my way or the highway" type.
   - ☐ A person who shows confidence in his or her direction.
   - ☐ A person who is a team-builder, who builds consensus.
   - ☐ A person with a record of success.
   - ☐ A person who is published or has a high degree in his or her field.
   - ☐ Other _____.

LEADER: Select three members of the group ahead of time to read aloud the Scripture passage. Have one member read the part of Mark, the narrator; another the part of Jesus; and the third person the part of the man with an unclean spirit. Ask the whole group to read the part of the crowd in verse 27. Then discuss the Questions for Interaction, dividing into subgroups of three to six.

Perhaps the area of biblical life that the rational mind has the greatest difficulty with is the references to evil and demonic spirits. And yet at the time of Jesus it was assumed that such beings existed, and that they could take hold of a person for destructive purposes. Jesus' mastery of these beings showed that there was nothing he could not conquer, and hence nothing in this world or any other world that we need to fear if we are in Christ. Read Mark 1:21-28, and note what happened as a result of this miracle.

Jesus Drives Out an Evil Spirit

Mark: [21]Then they went into Capernaum, and right away He entered the synagogue on the Sabbath and began to teach. [22]They were astonished at His teaching because, unlike the scribes, He was teaching them as one having authority. [23]Just then a man with an unclean spirit was in their synagogue. He cried out,

Man: [24]"What do You have to do with us, Jesus—Nazarene? Have You come to destroy us? I know who You are—the Holy One of God!"

Mark: [25]But Jesus rebuked him and said,

Jesus: "Be quiet, and come out of him!"

Mark: [26]And the unclean spirit convulsed him, shouted with a loud voice, and came out of him. [27]Then they were all amazed, so they began to argue with one another, saying,

Crowd: "What is this? A new teaching with authority! He commands even the unclean spirits, and they obey Him."

Mark: [28]His fame then spread throughout the entire vicinity of Galilee.

                                                            Mark 1:21-28

LEADER: Refer to the Summary and Study Notes at the end of this section as needed. If 30 minutes is not enough time to answer all of the questions in this section, conclude the Bible Study by answering question 7.

1. What is your dominant feeling when you think of stories in the Bible about evil spirits?
   - ❑ Curiosity.
   - ❑ Fear.
   - ❑ Excitement.
   - ❑ Disgust.
   - ❑ Incredulity.
   - ❑ Confusion.
   - ❑ Acceptance.
   - ❑ Other _____.

2. What things are implied when it is said that Jesus taught with "authority"?

3. Since the demon correctly identified Jesus, why might Jesus have ordered it to "be quiet" ?

4. This is the first miracle recorded in Mark. What might Mark want to show about Jesus in this initial demonstration of his power?

5. Have you ever experienced an evil in yourself or someone else that was so intense or so incomprehensible that you considered the possibility of demonic possession?

6. Given your understanding and experience of Jesus, what are a couple of things about him or his teachings that leave you "astonished" (v. 22)?

7. Jesus used his authority to bring freedom and wholeness to this man. In what ways have you experienced Jesus' authority doing the same in your life? What area of your life still needs the freedom and wholeness that only Jesus can bring?

GOING DEEPER: If your group has time and/or wants a challenge, go on to this question.

8. What is the relation between what modern science calls mental illness and what the Bible calls demon possession? Are they the same or two different realities? Should exorcism be considered in cases of bizarre or destructive behavior?

LEADER: Bring the group back together and begin the Caring Time by sharing responses to all three questions. Then take turns sharing prayer requests and having a time of group prayer. Be sure to include prayer for the empty chair.

Gather around each other now in this time of sharing and prayer. Remember that nothing is impossible with God, and he has given you the Holy Spirit to help you pray according to his will.

1. On a scale of 1 (none) to 10 (total), how much authority do you allow Jesus Christ to have in your life? What would have to be "cast out" of your life to raise your rating to a "10"? How can this group be supportive of you in this process?

2. Do you know someone who is having emotional or behavioral problems, whether psychological or demonic in origin? How can this group pray for these people?

3. Pray that Jesus would bring freedom and wholeness to each group member in the areas of life discussed in question 7.

   P.S. Add new group members to the Group Directory at the front of this book.

NEXT WEEK

Today we considered Jesus' miracle of driving an evil spirit out of a man, bringing him wholeness and freedom. In the coming week, ask the Holy Spirit to show you how evil may have a hold on you in certain areas of your life. Then pray for Jesus to free you from this evil. Next week we will talk about a man with leprosy whom Jesus healed, and how that man went on to tell everyone what Jesus had done for him. His story illustrates well what happens when we share what Jesus has done for us.

Summary: With his four newly chosen disciples present (1:16–20), Jesus' first public act of ministry recorded by Mark occurs in a synagogue. Here, with God's chosen people assembled, Jesus makes his presence known by the quality of his teaching and by his extraordinary power over demonic forces.

1:21 Capernaum. This was a town on the north end of the Sea of Galilee, three miles west of the River Jordan. It was a center of the fishing industry and the site of a custom's post. **synagogue.** In first-century Israel, the temple in Jerusalem was the sole site for sacrifices and was attended by numerous priests and other officials. In contrast, there were synagogues in each population center that people attended each week for worship and instruction. Synagogues were run by lay committees with no professional clergy attached to them. Anyone could speak as long as they had permission from the leaders.

1:22 astonished. Throughout the Gospel of Mark, Jesus' words and actions provoke amazement and surprise among the people. Here was something new that challenged accepted ways of thinking and living. Jesus' words and actions were pointers to the kingdom he was establishing, a kingdom that called for a response of repentance and faith from those wishing to be part of it (Mark 1:15). **at His teaching.** Mark records very little of Jesus' teaching in his gospel. Essentially, Jesus' message is summed up in 1:15: "the kingdom of God has come near. Repent and believe in the good news!" **as one having authority.** The teachers of the Law were men schooled in the interpretation of the Law and were responsible for helping the people in general understand and apply the Law in their situations. Their authority lay in their ability to quote the teachings of previous rabbis on the subject at hand. In contrast, Jesus taught directly. An example is seen in Matthew's version of the Sermon on the Mount in which Jesus counters traditional teaching with his repeated statement, "But I tell you ..." (Matt. 5:22,28,32,34,39,44) without the use of quotes from earlier rabbis to back him up. Jesus didn't need to quote human authorities because his authority was directly from God, and because he was God.

1:23 an unclean spirit. The Gospels frequently refer to these malignant, supernatural beings, able to harm and even possess people. We are not told what manifestation this spirit exhibited in this man's life, but from other stories in the New Testament we learn that a demonic spirit's activity can range from giving people a supernatural ability to foresee the future (Acts 16:16), to leading people to destructive, violent behaviors (5:1–5; 9:17). While not all sickness or bizarre behavior was attributed to the work of evil spirits, such ailments were thought to be common manifestations of possession by a spirit. In overcoming this evil spirit, Jesus demonstrated his power over Satan. He has come to bind the strong man (3:27), freeing people for God. The kingdom of God will be marked by the absence of such destructive forces.

1:24 I know who You are. By identifying Jesus, first using his human name and then by his divine title, the demon may have been trying to rely on ancient magical practices in the hope of gaining mastery over Jesus. It was believed that knowledge of a person's true identity (or secret name) gave one power over that person. Since the demon named Jesus, supposedly he would have Jesus in his power. However, such a tactic did not work with Jesus. **the Holy One of God!** The evil (unclean) spirit recognizes Jesus for who he is–the divine Son of God. In contrast, it will be quite some time before anyone else, including the disciples, understands this.

1:25 rebuked him. The same word is used in 4:39 when Jesus orders the tumult of the sea and wind to be still. The intent of the word is to show Jesus as the one who has authority to control and restrain the forces leading to chaos. **Be quiet.** Far from being overcome by the demon's ability to name him, Jesus orders the demon to be silent. This is yet another way in which Jesus asserts his authority over the demon. Throughout the Gospels, Jesus does not allow the demons to bear witness to him.

1:27 Mark notes the two things about Jesus that caught the attention of the people: the quality of his teaching and the power of his actions. **amazed.** See note on verse 22, where this word was translated "astonished." The amazement here is not over the presence of the man with a demon in their midst, since that would not have been an unexpected phenomenon for people of this day. What amazed them was Jesus' power over the demon. Such amazement contains not only joy but some alarm and even fear. Who is this man who possesses such unsuspected power?

1:28 His fame then spread. The people had witnessed amazing power and heard extraordinary teaching, and so it is not at all surprising that they told everyone they met what had happened in the synagogue. Jesus' power over the spirits led him to become a sought-after person in the region (1:32; 2:1–2; 3:7–10).

SESSION 3 : A MAN WITH LEPROSY

SCRIPTURE MARK 1:40-45

LAST WEEK

In last week's session, we considered how Jesus has authority over evil, and we looked at a time when Jesus drove an evil spirit out of a man. We were reminded of how Jesus still wants to bring freedom and wholeness to every area of our lives. This week we will focus on a healing miracle that Jesus performed on a man with leprosy, and how that man went on to tell everyone what Jesus had done for him.

ICE-BREAKER : CONNECT WITH YOUR GROUP | 15 MINUTES

LEADER: Choose one or two Ice-Breaker questions. If you have a new group member, you may want to do all three to help him or her get acquainted. Remember to stick closely to the three-part agenda and the time allowed for each segment.

Jesus often risked catching bad infections like leprosy in order to love people. But not all "infections" are bad. What "infections" have you been part of spreading? Share some of your own experiences and feelings by answering the following questions.

1. What was the most "infectious" thing about you when you were a teenager?
   - ☐ My smile.
   - ☐ My faith.
   - ☐ My negativism.
   - ☐ My gossip.
   - ☐ My friendliness.
   - ☐ My volcanic temper.
   - ☐ Other _____.

2. When have you felt as if you had an infectious disease that made everyone not want to be near you?

   ❑ When I went through a divorce and my married friends avoided me.

   ❑ When I was the new kid at school and the other kids ignored me.

   ❑ When I was a teenager with acne.

   ❑ When I actually had a disease.

   ❑ Other _____.

3. What would you most like to "infect" the world with right now?

   ❑ An epidemic of love.

   ❑ A widespread case of old-fashioned values.

   ❑ A feverish spreading of justice.

   ❑ An outbreak of faith.

   ❑ Other _____.

BIBLE STUDY : READ SCRIPTURE AND DISCUSS | 30 MINUTES

LEADER: Select a member of the group ahead of time to read aloud the Scripture passage. Then discuss the Questions for Interaction, dividing into subgroups of three to six.

Having already cured a man of a spiritual ailment, as we saw last week, Jesus went on to cure a person of a physical ailment. When he did, the man's amazement and feeling of thanksgiving was so great that he couldn't help telling everyone about it, even when Jesus cautioned him not to. Read Mark 1:40–45, and note what happened as a result of the man's testimony.

Jesus Heals a Man With Leprosy

⁴⁰Then a man with a serious skin disease came to Him and, on his knees, begged Him: "If You are willing, You can make me clean." ⁴¹Moved with compassion, Jesus reached out His hand and touched him. "I am willing," He told him. "Be made clean." ⁴²Immediately the disease left him, and he was healed. ⁴³Then He sternly warned him and sent him away at once, ⁴⁴telling him, "See that you say nothing to anyone; but go and show yourself to the priest, and offer what Moses prescribed for your cleansing, as a testimony to them." ⁴⁵Yet he went out and began to proclaim it widely and to spread the news, with the result that Jesus could no longer enter a town openly. But He was out in deserted places, and they would come to Him from everywhere.

Mark 1:40–45

QUESTIONS FOR INTERACTION

LEADER: Refer to the Summary and Study Notes at the end of this section as needed. If 30 minutes is not enough time to answer all of the questions in this section, conclude the Bible Study by answering question 7.

1. When have you found close contact with another person to be a healing experience for you? Conversely, when do you feel that you don't want to have contact with anyone?

2. Given that no one ever touched a leper, what is significant about Jesus' touch that, combined with his words, brought healing? What effect do you suppose this touch had on the leper?

3. The early church used these stories as illustrations of how Jesus frees people from sin. What parallels between leprosy and sin come to your mind as you consider their effect in the life of a person?

4. How do you account for Jesus' commands to the man in verse 44?

5. Why do you think the man ignored Jesus' warning about not telling anyone?
   - ☐ He was too excited to be quiet.
   - ☐ It was obvious that something had happened and he had to tell people.
   - ☐ Telling people might keep them from treating him as a leper.
   - ☐ He was probably in such a cloud from being healed that he didn't even hear the warning.
   - ☐ Other _____.

6. The call to silence was a temporary measure for a particular purpose. Typically, the Scripture calls us to tell others of God's good work in our lives. What is one thing that God has done for you for which you are particularly grateful? Who could you encourage by sharing this news? How could you do so?

7. Jesus risked both his health and his reputation by touching this man. What groups of people have you taken a risk in reaching out to? How has God met you as you took that risk? What risks are before you now in terms of reaching out to others?

GOING DEEPER: If your group has time and/or wants a challenge, go on to this question.

8. Who are the social outcasts and the "lepers" in our society? What role should Christians take in helping them to find acceptance and healing?

CARING TIME : APPLY THE LESSON AND PRAY FOR ONE ANOTHER | 15 MIN.

LEADER: Begin the Caring Time by having group members take turns sharing responses to all three questions. Be sure to save at least the last five minutes for a time of group prayer. Remember to include prayer for the empty chair when concluding the prayer time.

Encouraging and supporting each other is especially vital if this group is to become all it can be. Take time now to build up one another with sharing and prayer.

1. What is the best thing that happened to you last week? What is the worst?

2. What "lepers" would you especially like to remember in prayer?

3. How do you need Jesus' healing touch right now? How can the group support you in prayer?

NEXT WEEK

Today we saw how Jesus cares about our physical needs, in addition to our spiritual needs. We focused on a man with leprosy whom Jesus healed, and considered how that man went on to tell everyone what Jesus had done for him. In the coming week, share with at least one other person something miraculous that God has done for you. Next week we will examine the healing of a paralytic who was carried to Jesus by four friends, and how this encourages us, as Christians, to be supportive of one another.

Summary: Mark ends the first chapter of his gospel with an account of a powerful healing. This is the first of three stories in Mark that lead to Jesus' declaration of his mission as having come as a doctor "not for the healthy ... but the sick" (2:17). In this story, Jesus deals with a man with an obvious physical problem. Leprosy serves as a particularly apt illustration of sin and evil. Like sin, it brings progressive physical and psychological disintegration, it disfigures both body and soul, it alienates people from one another, it leads those it infects to despise their own selves and it cuts people off from the worship of God (since lepers were forbidden from coming to the temple). Perhaps most tragically, like sin, it was beyond one's ability to change. This miracle implies that in the presence of Jesus, sin, like this man's leprosy, no longer has the final word about a person's destiny.

1:40 a serious skin disease. This is generally said to be leprosy. No disease was dreaded more than leprosy since it brought not only physical disfigurement but, because of fear of contamination, social banishment as well. At this time, leprosy was a word used to describe not only the true leprosy known today as Hansen's disease, but was applied to a wide range of serious skin diseases. While the Old Testament Law called for banishment of lepers, in Jesus' day lepers were prohibited only from living in Jerusalem and a few other ancient cities. Although lepers could live where they wanted, they were considered religiously unclean. Thus, the rabbis developed elaborate regulations regarding how they were to be avoided in order to maintain one's ritual purity. This underlined their social isolation and sense of self-hatred. **came to Him.** What the leper did was forbidden by law. The leper should have sought to avoid drawing near Jesus so as not to render him religiously unclean. The rabbis taught that if a leper passed by a clean man, the clean man would not become unclean. However, if the leper stopped, then the clean man could become unclean.

1:41 Moved with compassion. Human suffering evoked a deep, affective response from Jesus. He was not afraid of strong emotions. This affective response also shows that his miracles were not just a strategy to demonstrate who he was. They were an expression of his compassion as well. **reached out His hand and touched him.** Actually touching a leper was unimaginable to most first-century people. Not only did one risk contracting the disease, but such contact made the healthy person ritually impure and thus unable to participate in the religious life of the community. By this gesture, Jesus showed his lack of concern for the details of religious tradition when they came into conflict with human need.

1:42 Immediately. This is a favorite word for Mark. In this context it shows the immediacy and efficacy of Jesus' word. It is reminiscent of the word of God in creation as seen in Genesis 1 in which "and God said ..." is immediately followed by "... and it was so."

1:43 Then He sternly warned him and sent him away at once. While the parallel stories in Luke and Matthew report how Jesus ordered him not to tell others, they lack the strength of the term Mark uses here. It may be that this reflects more closely an eyewitness account of the event. The stern charge was to prevent what did indeed end up happening.

27

The man did tell others, resulting in Jesus' inability to continue his preaching ministry as he intended.

1:44 See that you say nothing to anyone. Throughout the Gospels, Jesus repeatedly urges those who have experienced a private miracle not to tell others, the one exception being the demoniac in 5:19. That exception to the rule offers the insight to explain the call to silence. The demoniac was a Gentile in a Gentile environment. In that context, where there were no messianic expectations, the word could be freely spread that God was doing something even for Gentiles in and through this Jewish man. While that might arouse interest, it would not fuel the political fires that news of the Messiah would (and did) fuel in Israel. John 6:15 shows how quickly the political hopes of Israel for deliverance from Rome could be stirred up. While this was the popular expectation of the Messiah, it was not an expectation Jesus intended to fulfill. Jesus was the Messiah, but not this kind of military Messiah. He needed time to communicate what kind of Messiah he was, one that came to die—not to conquer by force. Eventually, the time for secrecy would be over, but at this early point in his ministry he did not want to rouse false hopes that would make his true mission difficult. **offer what Moses prescribed.** In Leviticus 14:1–32, the ritual is outlined whereby a leper is declared "clean." Such certification was vital to a leper: it was that person's way back into human society. This also shows Jesus' respect for the Law. **as a testimony to them.** This refers to the priests. Since they were the ones who had to verify a person's cleansing, they would have made an official pronouncement of his healing. Thus, the healing would have been a testimony because it would be clear evidence that God was indeed at work in and through Jesus. The rabbis considered curing leprosy as difficult as raising someone from the dead. In the Old Testament, only Moses and Elisha ever successfully cured someone of leprosy. If the priest acknowledged that Jesus had indeed cured this man's leprosy, it would have been powerful evidence to them of his divine authority.

1:45 proclaim it widely and to spread the news. Jesus' command was ignored. The leper's joy could not be contained as he told everyone how he came to be healed. The terms used here are common words used later on in the New Testament to describe the nature and content of Christian preaching. **Jesus could no longer enter a town openly.** His teaching ministry (1:38) was hindered by the clamor of people coming to him only for exorcisms and healings. While they were a sign of what he had come to do, his real mission was to pronounce the deliverance from sin for those who would repent and seek after God's kingdom (1:15; 2:17).

SESSION 4 : JESUS HEALS A PARALYTIC

SCRIPTURE MARK 2:1-12

Our focus in last week's session was on Jesus' healing of a man with leprosy. We saw how Jesus was willing to reach out to someone who was considered unclean and shunned by society. We were reminded that Jesus cares about our physical needs, in addition to our spiritual needs. This week we will look at another physical healing, and see how important friends can be in leading us to Christ and building us up in the faith.

ICE-BREAKER : CONNECT WITH YOUR GROUP | 15 MINUTES

LEADER: Welcome and introduce new group members. Choose one, two or all three of the Ice-Breaker questions.

In today's world of great scientific and medical advances, it's hard to believe in miraculous healing. Most of us search for logical answers and solutions to unexplainable events. Take turns sharing your unique experiences with times you needed health care.

1. \What does your family do when you are sick?
   - ☐ Say, "Poor baby!"
   - ☐ Pump me full of vitamins.
   - ☐ Pamper me and tend to my every need.
   - ☐ Tell me to "suck it up."
   - ☐ Ignore me.
   - ☐ Have me take care of *them* .
   - ☐ Other _____.

2. When was the last time you had to go to the emergency room? Who took you there and how were you treated once you got there?

3. Share a story of a time when you felt God miraculously intervened to heal someone.

29

When Jesus healed a person, he normally referred to that person's faith as an important factor in the healing. In the following story, however, the text refers to the faith of the man and his friends as being most important. This shows us the importance of supporting one another in our efforts to find healing. Read Mark 2:1-12, and note how Jesus healed the paralytic both spiritually and physically.

Jesus Heals a Paralytic

2 When He entered Capernaum again after some days, it was reported that He was at home. [2] So many people gathered together that there was no more room, even near the door, and He was speaking the message to them. [3] Then they came to Him bringing a paralytic, carried by four men. [4] Since they were not able to bring him to Jesus because of the crowd, they removed the roof above where He was. And when they had broken through, they lowered the stretcher on which the paralytic was lying.

[5] Seeing their faith, Jesus told the paralytic, "Son, your sins are forgiven."

[6] But some of the scribes were sitting there, reasoning in their hearts: [7] "Why does He speak like this? He's blaspheming! Who can forgive sins but God alone?"

[8] Right away Jesus understood in His spirit that they were reasoning like this within themselves, and said to them, "Why are you reasoning these things in your hearts? [9] Which is easier: to say to the paralytic, 'Your sins are forgiven,' or to say, 'Get up, pick up your stretcher, and walk'? [10] But so you may know that the Son of Man has authority on earth to forgive sins," He told the paralytic, [11] "I tell you: get up, pick up your stretcher, and go home."

[12] Immediately he got up, picked up the stretcher, and went out in front of everyone. As a result, they were all astounded and gave glory to God, saying, "We have never seen anything like this!"

Mark 2:1-12

QUESTIONS FOR INTERACTION

LEADER: Refer to the Summary and Study Notes at the end of this section as needed. If 30 minutes is not enough time to answer all of the questions in this section, conclude the Bible Study by answering question 7.

1. If something like this happened on Sunday in your church, what would people say?
   - ☐ "Okay, take that sort of thing to the church down the street!"
   - ☐ "Who is going to pay for the roof?"
   - ☐ "Let's not get carried away."
   - ☐ "This is going to mean the service will go past 12:00!"
   - ☐ "Praise God!"
   - ☐ "How about the rest of us 'paralytics'?"
   - ☐ Other _____.

2. What do you think was going on in the minds of the following persons as the events of verses 1–4 unfolded?
   - The paralytic.
   - His four friends.
   - The owner of the house.
   - Jesus.

3. What impresses you the most about the four friends in the story?

4. The man obviously was brought for healing. Why did Jesus first bring up the whole issue of sin and forgiveness?

5. In the last session, sin was compared to leprosy. In what ways have you experienced sin to be like paralysis?

6. How have you experienced Jesus' saying to you personally that "your sins are forgiven" (v. 5)? What freedom has that brought to you?

7. If you had friends who took you to Jesus for healing today, what kind of healing would you need—physical, spiritual, emotional, relational? What is the greatest obstacle your friends would have to help you overcome?

GOING DEEPER: If your group has time and/or wants a challenge, go on to this question.

8. Jesus tells the paralytic that his sins are forgiven. Is there a connection between sin and physical disease?

CARING TIME : APPLY THE LESSON AND PRAY FOR ONE ANOTHER | 15 MIN.

LEADER: Be sure to save at least 15 minutes for this important time. After sharing responses to all three questions and asking for prayer requests, close in a time of group prayer.

Following the example of the paralytic's friends, take some time now to encourage and support one another in your faith. Begin by discussing the following questions, and then share prayer requests.

1. What does this group need to be doing to show to each other the same kind of support that the four friends showed for this paralytic? Pray that the group might be better able to follow these friends' example.

2. Take some time to thank God for forgiving your sins and giving you the gift of eternal life.

3. Pray for God's strength to help the person on your right to get past the obstacles he or she reported in question 7.

NEXT WEEK

Today we rejoiced with the paralytic as he received spiritual and physical healing from Jesus. We saw how the paralytic's healing probably would not have taken place, were it not for the love and concern of his friends. Next week we will consider the story of Jesus' miraculous feeding of over five thousand people, and what this has to say to us about God's provision.

Summary: Whereas in the story of the leper, Jesus only dealt with the man's physical need, here he deliberately introduces the issue of spiritual need. While everyone waits to see if Jesus can heal the paralytic, he brings up an unexpected discussion about sin and forgiveness. Like leprosy, paralysis also serves as a powerful illustration of sin. Sin deadens one's ability to function normally. It leaves people spiritually incapable of walking in God's ways and unable to respond to God's invitations. People are not naturally healed of its effects.

Since the news about Jesus has spread everywhere (1:28,45), it is not surprising that the religious leaders want to know who he is and what he stands for. This is the first of five stories in which the religious authorities probe his orthodoxy, a probing that ends in their resolve to kill him (3:6).

2:1 at home. Capernaum served as Jesus' base for his travels in Galilee. Quite possibly this was the home of Peter and Andrew (1:29,32–33).

2:2 He was speaking the message to them. Although Mark does not record much of Jesus' preaching, he continually points out that announcing the news of the kingdom was Jesus' main agenda (1:14–15,38; 2:13; 3:14; 4:1; 6:2,12,34).

2:3 a paralytic. Luke, the doctor, uses (in Greek) a technically more exact phrase to describe this man's illness (Luke 5:18). From that we understand that he was, apparently, a paraplegic with spinal damage.

2:4 they removed the roof. The roof of a typical Palestinian house was flat (it was often used for sleeping) and was reached by an outside ladder or stairway. It was constructed of earth and brushwood that was packed between wooden beams set about three feet apart. The roof would not have been entirely removed, but rather an opening would have been made in this packing. This type of roof was easily opened up (and could easily be repaired). A rather large opening would have been required to lower a man on a mat. While this was going on, with the noise and falling dirt, all attention inside would have been diverted from Jesus' sermon to the ever-growing hole.

2:5 Seeing their faith. Jesus' act of forgiveness and healing is connected to faith. In this case it is the faith of the paralytic's friends. Their faith was shown in the fact that they brought the paralytic and they overcame in a very clever, determined way the obstacle that prevented them from bringing their friend to Jesus. **your sins are forgiven.** The popular thought of the time was that all disease and misfortune was a punishment for sin, and so this connection of paralysis to sin would not have been entirely unexpected. In John 9:1–3, Jesus' disciples ask a question concerning whether a certain man born blind was born that way because of the sin of his parents or his own sin. They assume it must have been someone's sin. Jesus tells them that it was not a matter of punishment for sin, but so that God might display his work in his life. Jesus is not, then saying that this paralytic was paralyzed because of his sin. However, it is likely that the man was wrestling with guilt because of the popular conception. He probably thought of hundreds of things he had done wrong (as we all could) that might have caused this misfortune. Jesus wanted him to know that he was forgiven of all these sins. Having said that, it should also be noted that modern science has connected many types of physical ailments with psychological and emotional factors. Even paralysis, in some rare instances, is related to unresolved feelings of guilt. And so it is also possible that something like this was operational in this man's case.

2:6 scribes. These are the teachers of the Law, religious lawyers who interpreted Jewish law. Originally, it was their job to make copies of the Old Testament. Because of their familiarity with Scripture, people consulted them about points of law and hence their role evolved into that of teacher and protector of the Law. Luke's account of this story (5:17–26) states that the scribes had come from "every village of Galilee and from Judea and Jerusalem" indicating that this was an official delegation sent to investigate the orthodoxy of this unknown, enormously popular teacher.

2:7 blaspheming. Blasphemy is the act of expressing contempt for God or usurping the rights of God. Under Jewish law its penalty is death (Lev. 24:16). The scribes also believed in the popular idea that illness was the direct result of sin, so that the sick could not recover until their sin had been forgiven by God. However, they also knew that God alone could offer forgiveness. Hence, they are distressed that Jesus has said to the paralytic, "your sins are forgiven." This was to claim in quite explicit terms that he was divine, and this was the vilest blasphemy.

2:10 But so you may know ... to forgive sins. If Jesus is able to heal the paralytic, the scribes would have to admit that he had indeed the power to forgive sins, since their own theology linked forgiveness and healing. The visible healing would verify the invisible forgiveness. **the Son of Man.** This is Mark's first use of this title, going back to Daniel 7:13–14 in which the prophet Daniel sees a vision of one "like a son of man" receiving authority to rule over God's kingdom.

2:12 they were all astounded. Mark's miracle stories usually end with an observation of the amazement of those who witnessed them. The "all" would not seem to include the scribes who from this time on became more and more resistant to Jesus.

SESSION 5 : JESUS FEEDS THE FIVE THOUSAND

SCRIPTURE MARK 6:30-44

LAST WEEK

The spiritual and physical healing of the paralytic was the miracle we focused on in last week's session. We saw the importance of the support of friends in overcoming. We were reminded how we need each other on our journey of faith. This week we will consider the story of Jesus' miraculous feeding of over five thousand people, and what this has to say to us about God's provision.

ICE-BREAKER : CONNECT WITH YOUR GROUP | 15 MINUTES

LEADER: Open with a word of prayer, and then introduce any new people or visitors. To help new group members get acquainted, remember to do all three Ice-Breaker questions.

Jesus was host at perhaps one of the biggest picnics ever. After feeding thousands, he had plenty left over for future meals. Share some of your own thoughts and experiences with picnics and leftovers.

1. At large church or family picnics, what food do you usually go for right away?
   - ◻ The hot dogs and hamburgers.
   - ◻ Fried chicken.
   - ◻ Watermelon.
   - ◻ The chips and dip.
   - ◻ The pie or cake—"I always eat dessert first!"
   - ◻ Other _____.

2. If someone could provide you with an endless supply of one food, what food would you choose?

3. What is your family policy in regard to "leftovers"?
   - ◻ Keep them until they add to our collection of green mold in the refrigerator.
   - ◻ Use them for lunch the next day.
   - ◻ Give them to the smallest kid, who can't defend himself.
   - ◻ Don't even bother—toss everything in the disposal.
   - ◻ Label them and use them within a few days.
   - ◻ Other _____.

LEADER: Select three members of the group ahead of time to read aloud the Scripture passage. Have one person read the part of Mark, the narrator; another person the part of Jesus; and a third person to read the part of the disciples. Then discuss the Questions for Interaction, dividing into subgroups of three to six.

When one attracts large crowds of people by teaching and healing, there are certain practical problems that are created. Such was certainly true with Jesus. The thousands of people were so enthralled with his teaching that many of them apparently didn't even think of bringing something to eat. Yet Jesus used this as an opportunity to show his power to provide. Read Mark 6:30–44, and note how the disciples reacted to this situation.

Jesus Feeds the Five Thousand

Mark: [30]The apostles gathered around Jesus and reported to Him all that they had done and taught. [31]He said to them,

Jesus: "Come away by yourselves to a remote place and rest a little."

Mark: For many people were coming and going, and they did not even have time to eat. [32]So they went away in the boat by themselves to a remote place, [33]but many saw them leaving and recognized them. Then they ran there on foot from all the towns and arrived ahead of them. [34]So as He stepped ashore, He saw a huge crowd and had compassion on them, because they were like sheep without a shepherd. Then He began to teach them many things. [35]When it was already late, His disciples approached Him and said,

Disciples: "This place is a wilderness, and the hour is already late! [36]Send them away, so they can go into the surrounding countryside and villages to buy themselves something to eat."

Jesus: [37]"You give them something to eat," He responded.

Disciples: They said to Him, "Should we go and buy 200 denarii worth of bread and give them something to eat?"

Jesus: [38]And He asked them, "How many loaves do you have? Go look."

Disciples: When they found out they said, "Five, and two fish."

Mark: [39]Then He instructed them to have all the people sit down in groups on the green grass. [40]So they sat down in ranks of hundreds and fifties. [41]Then He took the five loaves and the two fish, and looking up to heaven, He blessed and broke the loaves. And He kept giving them to His disciples to set before the people. He also divided the two fish among them all. [42]Everyone ate and was filled. [43]Then they picked up 12 baskets full of pieces of bread and fish. [44]Now those who ate the loaves were 5,000 men.

Mark 6:30–44

QUESTIONS FOR INTERACTION

LEADER: Refer to the Summary and Study Notes at the end of this section as needed. If 30 minutes is not enough time to answer all of the questions in this section, conclude the Bible Study by answering questions 6 and 7.

1. When you need to get away to a quiet place, where do you go, and what do you do while there?
   - ❏ I go to an empty church and pray.
   - ❏ I find a peaceful place in nature and listen for God's guidance.
   - ❏ I go to a special room in my house and study God's Word.
   - ❏ Other _____.

2. Jesus said, "Come away by yourselves to a remote place and rest a little" (v. 31). If you were one of the disciples, how would you have felt when you got there and thousands of people were waiting for you?

3. What attitudes and emotions do you sense in the disciples' response when Jesus tells them to feed the crowd?

4. What connection do you see between this story and the Lord's Supper?

5. Mark makes no mention of the disciples' reaction to what happened. If you were one of the Twelve, what thoughts would be running through your mind as you went about picking up the leftovers from what seemed to be a terribly scanty meal? What was the lesson to be learned?

6. What monumental task are you facing right now that seems most like trying to feed thousands of people? What are the "five loaves and two fish" provided to you as resources to meet this challenge?

7. Where might Jesus be telling you to respond to his call to "give something to eat" to the people in need around you?

GOING DEEPER: If your group has time and/or wants a challenge, go on to this question.

8. This story is full of Old Testament allusions (Num. 27:15–17; Ps. 23:1–2; Ezek. 34:11–15). In light of this background, what does this event reveal about Jesus?

CARING TIME : APPLY THE LESSON AND PRAY FOR ONE ANOTHER | 15 MIN.

LEADER: Encourage everyone to participate in this important time and be sure that each group member is receiving prayer support. Continue to pray for the empty chair in the closing group prayer.

Comfort and encourage one another with this time of sharing and prayer. Begin by sharing your responses to the following questions. Be sure to offer any other prayer requests and concerns before closing in prayer.

1. Where are you in the journey of following Christ?
   ❏ I am a seeker.
   ❏ I have just begun the journey.
   ❏ I'm returning after getting lost on the wrong path.
   ❏ I've been following Christ for a long time.
   ❏ Other _____.

2. How can you pray for the people in your neighborhood who are like sheep without a shepherd?

3. How can this group support you in prayer in relation to the monumental task you talked about in question 6?

NEXT WEEK

Today we were reminded of the great compassion that Jesus has for us as we seek to know him better. We focused on his miraculous feeding of over five thousand people, and saw how he wants to meet our every need. In the coming week, go to Jesus with your needs and seek his wisdom and guidance on using what you already have to meet those needs. Next week we will examine a time when Jesus calmed a storm that seemed to threaten the lives of his followers, and how Jesus can calm our "storms" as well.

Summary: This passage of Scripture comes in the midst of two parallel cycles of stories. The point is made in both cycles that it will take a miracle from Jesus to heal the hardened hearts of the Twelve so that they can come to see who he really is—or at least to understand as much as they can, prior to his death and resurrection. Cycle one (6:30–7:37) begins with the feeding of the five thousand and ends with a healing of a deaf and dumb man. Cycle two (8:1–25) begins with the feeding of the four thousand and ends with the healing of a blind man. In both cases, the reader is shown the inability of the disciples to understand what is happening. It is as if they are deaf, dumb and blind.

6:30 Having returned from their mission to preach, cast out demons and heal in the villages throughout Galilee (vv. 7–13), the Twelve report to the Lord what took place in their travels. **apostles.** This is the only time this term is used in Mark. Here it is not so much a title as a description of what they have just done. An apostle is "one who is sent" and they have just completed the missionary work the Lord sent them out to do (v. 7).

6:33 ran there on foot. The crowds are now wise to the disciples' tactic of simply sailing off across the lake and leaving them standing on the shore (4:35–36). So they follow on foot. The distances would not have been great since the lake was only eight miles at its widest. As they run around the lake to get to the place where the boats would land, more and more people from the lakeside villages would join with them, swelling their numbers.

6:34 sheep without a shepherd. Without a shepherd, sheep are hopelessly lost. They have no way to defend themselves and they will probably starve. This was an apt metaphor for the condition of the crowd. They had been abandoned, by and large, by the religious leaders. Their inability to keep the oral law caused them to be considered "unclean" in a religious sense. This phrase itself is taken from the Old Testament and is one of several Old Testament allusions Mark uses to hint to the reader that the miracle is really intended to show that Jesus is God with us, the True Shepherd of Israel.

6:35 a wilderness. This is the third reference to a wilderness area (vv. 31–32). This is an allusion to Moses who led the people of Israel in the wilderness. Jesus makes this connection very strong in John 6:26–51.

6:36 Send them away. This is the disciples' solution. "Let the people buy what they need in the nearby towns." This is not a reasonable suggestion if the situation is viewed in ordinary terms, for there are too many people for the supplies available in the local villages. In addition, some of the people may have been too poor to purchase food.

6:37 You give them something to eat. Jesus has quite a different solution in mind. The response of the disciples indicates that they had no clue as to how Jesus expected them to do this. Jesus' statement, and the entire scene, is similar to that found in 2 Kings 4:42–44. In that situation, Elisha, a great prophet of the Lord, miraculously provided food for 100 people from 20 loaves of bread. If the people saw that as an act authenticating Elisha's commission from God, how much more should they see the miracle Jesus is about to perform as an act confirming his divine authority? **200 denarii worth.** This would have been seven months' wages for the average working person. Once again, as during the storm on the lake (4:37–38), the disciples do not expect that Jesus will be able to solve the problem in a miraculous way. The only way they can see to feed the crowd is to buy lots of food.

6:41 five loaves. These were small round cakes made of wheat or barley. What Jesus does here is what Moses did in the wilderness: he feeds the hungry multitudes (Ex. 16; Num. 11). **two fish.** These were probably smoked or pickled fish. **blessed/broke/kept giving.** There are overtones here of the Last Supper (14:12–26) and the church's practice of Communion (1 Cor. 11:23–24). The words that Jesus uses parallel the words of institution taken from the description of the Last Supper: "Jesus took bread, gave thanks and broke it, and gave it to his disciples, saying, 'Take it; this is My body' " (14:22). This feeding, like the Lord's Supper, is a foreshadowing of the feeding of all God's people at the messianic banquet.

6:42 was filled. Miraculously, the five loaves and two fish fed everyone not meagerly but abundantly, so that they were filled. As in the scene with Elisha (2 Kin. 4:44), there was more than enough to go around, accenting God's lavish generosity.

6:44 men. Literally, this is "males." Matthew 14:21 makes it clear there were women and children present as well. The actual number of people fed far exceeded five thousand.

SESSION 6 : JESUS CALMS THE STORM

SCRIPTURE MARK 4:35–41

LAST WEEK

In last week's session, we considered Jesus' miraculous feeding of over five thousand people. We were reminded that Jesus has great compassion for us and wants to be our Shepherd and Guide as we journey through life. He also wants to provide for our needs in ways we can't imagine. This week we will focus on the power over nature that Jesus demonstrated when he calmed a violent storm that threatened the lives of his disciples. We will also see how Jesus wants to calm our "storms" as well.

ICE-BREAKER : CONNECT WITH YOUR GROUP | 15 MINUTES

LEADER: Choose one or two of the Ice-Breaker questions. If you have a new group member, you may want to do all three. Remember to stick closely to the three-part agenda and the time allowed for each segment.

It has been said that "into every life a little rain must fall." But it makes a big difference whether that rain comes gently or as part of a violent storm! Jesus and the disciples experienced a number of storms. Take turns sharing some of your unique experiences with storms and violent weather.

1. Where were you raised and how often did you experience violent storms? What kind of storm was most common?
   - ☐ Tornadoes.
   - ☐ Hurricanes.
   - ☐ Ice storms.
   - ☐ Snowstorms.
   - ☐ Other _____.

2. When you were a child, which of the following were you most likely to do during a bad storm?
   - ❑ Hop into bed with Mom and Dad.
   - ❑ Get in bed with an older sibling.
   - ❑ Hide under the covers.
   - ❑ Stay up and watch the lightning.
   - ❑ Head for the basement or storm shelter.
   - ❑ Other _____.

3. What is the most tumultuous weather event you have ever slept through?

BIBLE STUDY : READ SCRIPTURE AND DISCUSS | 30 MINUTES

LEADER: Select a member of the group ahead of time to read aloud the Scripture passage. Then discuss the Questions for Interaction, dividing into subgroups of three to six.

There is something about a thunderous storm that dredges up the most primitive fears of childhood. It often makes a person feel small and vulnerable. Perhaps that is how the disciples felt when they found themselves in a storm one day. And to make matters worse, they were in a boat out in the middle of a lake when it happened. At such a time, you can really learn what your faith is made of. Unfortunately, the disciples found that their faith was lacking, as Jesus had to rescue them. Read Mark 4:35–41, and note how the disciples react to this miracle.

Jesus Calms the Storm

³⁵On that day, when evening had come, He told them, "Let's cross over to the other side of the lake" ³⁶So they left the crowd and took Him along since He was in the boat. And other boats were with Him. ³⁷A fierce windstorm arose, and the waves were breaking over the boat, so that the boat was already being swamped. ³⁸But He was in the stern, sleeping on the cushion. So they woke Him up and said to Him, "Teacher! Don't you care we're going to die?"

³⁹He got up, rebuked the wind, and said to the sea, "Silence! Be still!" The wind ceased, and there was a great calm. ⁴⁰Then He said to them, "Why are you fearful? Do you still have no faith?"

⁴¹And they were terrified and said to one another, "Who then is this? Even the wind and the sea obey Him!"

Mark 4:35–41

QUESTIONS FOR INTERACTION

LEADER: Refer to the Summary and Study Notes at the end of this section as needed. If 30 minutes is not enough time to answer all of the questions in this section, conclude the Bible Study by answering question 7.

1. If you had been one of the disciples when the boat was about to sink, what would you have done?
   - ❑ Jumped overboard.
   - ❑ Taken command.
   - ❑ Screamed for help.
   - ❑ Acted as if nothing was wrong.
   - ❑ Started bailing water.
   - ❑ Woke Jesus up.
   - ❑ Blamed God.
   - ❑ Other _____.

2. Why was Jesus sleeping through such a storm in the first place?
   - ❑ He was a sound sleeper.
   - ❑ He wanted to see how the disciples reacted on their own.
   - ❑ He had great trust in God, his Father.
   - ❑ He must have been really tired from all the work and stress.
   - ❑ Other _____.

3. Had you been in the boat with Jesus, what would your attitude have been toward the fact that he was sleeping while you fought this storm?
   - ❑ "What—is he too good to help us out with this?"
   - ❑ "Maybe he knows something we don't!"
   - ❑ "He's God's Son alright—we're in desperate trouble and he couldn't care less!"
   - ❑ "We've got to protect him!"
   - ❑ "If this is some kind of test, I'm failing miserably!"
   - ❑ "Wake him—he's our only hope!"
   - ❑ Other _____.

4. What was the tone in Jesus' voice when he said, "Why are you fearful?" Was he angry, disappointed, compassionate or just inquisitive?

5. What was the difference in the fear of the disciples during the storm and their fear at the end of the story? At the end of the story, do you think that the disciples were more afraid of the storm or of Jesus? Why?

6. When have you reacted with fear to something God has done? Is fearing God in this manner appropriate or inappropriate for a Christian?

7. When have you felt like the disciples in verse 38, wondering whether or not Jesus cared about the plight that was overtaking you? What happened? What did you learn through that experience?

43

If your group has time and/or wants a challenge, go on to this question.

8. When Christians hit stormy times in life, should they call upon the Lord right away, or try to handle it on their own first? What does God want us to do on our own, and what does he want us to rely on him for?

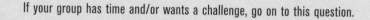

CARING TIME : APPLY THE LESSON AND PRAY FOR ONE ANOTHER | 15 MIN.

LEADER: Be sure to save at least 15 minutes for this time of prayer and encouragement. Continue to encourage group members to invite new people to the group. Remind them that this group is for learning and sharing, but also for reaching out to others.

Knowing that Jesus is able to calm any "storm" in your life, come before him now in this time of sharing and prayer. Encourage and support one another so you can have peace and not be afraid.

1. What is the immediate forecast for the "weather" in your life, and why?
   - ❏ Sunny and warm.
   - ❏ Overcast.
   - ❏ Chance for showers.
   - ❏ Partly cloudy.
   - ❏ Storm clouds are brewing.
   - ❏ Other _____

2. When do you remember Jesus helping you through a storm? What would you like to thank him for now in relation to that experience?

3. What stress or worry do you have right now that you need Jesus to calm? If Jesus were to say to you, "Silence! Be still," what would he mean?

NEXT WEEK

This week we considered the miracle that happened when Jesus calmed a storm and the disciples' fears. We were reminded how Jesus can calm our "storms" as well and bring peace and joy to our lives. In the coming week, write down your fears and worries on a piece of paper and pray about them daily. Then see how God acts in your life to bring you peace. Next week we will take a look at another miracle involving a demon-possessed man and how Jesus brought healing and wholeness to his life.

Summary: Now Jesus demonstrates his authority over the forces of nature and death. This is one of four stories in this section that unveil the unique, awesome power of Jesus. The disciples see that he has authority over the very elements of nature (vv. 35–41); over the most extreme case of possession by evil (5:1–20); over long-term, seemingly incurable disease (5:24–34); and even over death itself (5:21–24,35–43). Through these stories, Mark is showing that Jesus simply does not fit into any of the traditional categories of holy men or respected teachers. His works indicate that he is set apart from any rabbi or prophet.

4:36 other boats were with Him. Although these boats do not play any other role in the story, their mention, as well as that of other details not found in the parallel accounts (Matt. 8:23–27; Luke 8:22–25), indicate an eyewitness testimony of the event. Presumably the people in these boats were also saved when Jesus stilled the storm.

4:37 A fierce windstorm. The Sea of Galilee was a deep, freshwater lake, 13 miles long and eight miles wide at its widest point. It was pear-shaped and ringed by hills, though open at it north and south ends. Fierce winds blew into this bowl-shaped sea creating savage and unpredictable storms. **the waves were breaking over the boat, so that the boat was already being swamped.** In this succinct phrase Mark identifies the problem. The boat was filling with water. This reduced its maneuverability, and eventually would sink it. Bailing the water out of the boat was, therefore, of utmost importance.

4:38 sleeping. In the Old Testament sleeping peacefully is a sign of trust in the power of God (Ps. 4:8). The fact that Jesus was asleep during a storm is also a sign of his exhaustion from a day of teaching. **on the cushion.** This was probably a cushion used for the rowers to sit upon. **Don't you care we're going to die?** This is a rebuke. Jesus' rest in the midst of the storm was not seen as a sign of trust in God to protect and deliver him, but as a sign of his callousness toward the plight of the disciples. The disciples were scared. They woke him up simply so he could help them bail out the boat since it was about to be swamped (v. 37). As their later response indicates (v. 41), they had no expectation that he would have any power over the storm.

4:39 Instead of bailing, Jesus commands the wind and waves to be still—and they obey. Thus, he demonstrates his power over the very elements in the same way that God does (Ps. 65:7; 106:9). This was something no ordinary rabbi could do. **Silence!** This is literally, "Be muzzled!" as if the storm were some wild beast needing to be subdued. The same word was used to cast out the demon in the story in 1:25. This command to silence presses God's peace into the strife that fights against God and his ways. **a great calm.** This was a genuine miracle. When Jesus spoke it was not a matter of the wind beginning to slacken and the waves starting to die down. In one moment the Sea of Galilee was smooth and placid. What Jesus did here reflects God's power and authority over the sea (Ps. 65:7; 89:9; 106:9; 107:23–32). Perhaps the most vivid example of God's power over the sea was his opening of the Red Sea so that Israel could pass through.

4:40 fearful. Some of the disciples were fishermen who knew how serious their peril was in the face of the storm. Because of the danger, actual fear for their lives was not inappropriate. However, once Jesus displays his power, their fear of the storm turns into fear of

Jesus. This is the fear of the unknown and the unexplainable. The disciples were totally unprepared for this action. **Do you still have no faith?** Although Jesus had not yet performed any miracle of this nature, the disciples should have learned by now that nothing was impossible with him. This miracle would force the disciples to reconsider all they had heard and seen from Jesus: What had he said or done that should lead them to expect he could act like this?

4:41 terrified. Terror replaced fear. This is what is felt in the presence of an unknown force or power. It is the response a vision of a demon, angel, ghost or some other strange, supernatural experience would inspire. **Who then is this?** This is the key question. The congregation in the synagogue where Jesus did his first miracle in Mark wondered about this (1:27). The religious leaders asked this question (2:7; 3:22). Now his disciples discover that even they do not understand who he is. The rest of Mark describes how the disciples, in particular, overcome their culturally conditioned assumptions about who Jesus is and, step-by-step, discover his true nature.

SESSION 7 : HEALING A DEMON-POSSESSED MAN

SCRIPTURE MARK 5:1–20

LAST WEEK

The miracle of Jesus calming the storm was our focus in last week's session. We were reminded how Jesus wants to bring us peace and calm our "storms" as well. This week we will consider how Jesus brought peace and wholeness to another demon-possessed man. We will also see how this man couldn't help but share with others what Jesus had done for him.

ICE-BREAKER : CONNECT WITH YOUR GROUP | 15 MINUTES

LEADER: Open with a word of prayer, and then introduce and welcome any new group members. Choose one, two or all three Ice-Breaker questions to get started.

In Jesus' ministry on earth, he sometimes went to some pretty strange places and encountered some pretty strange characters. Share some of your own experiences with strange people and places.

1. What is the most interesting natural phenomenon you have ever seen?
   - ☐ Old Faithful in Yellowstone National Park.
   - ☐ The Badlands in South Dakota.
   - ☐ A tornado or hurricane.
   - ☐ The gentleness of a whale.
   - ☐ Salmon swimming upstream.
   - ☐ Other _____.

2. Who was the craziest friend you had in high school? What particularly weird things do you remember this person saying or doing?

3. When you meet someone today who is kind of strange, which of the following are you most likely to do?
   - ☐ Walk away quickly.
   - ☐ Stop and try to "figure the person out."
   - ☐ Feel sorry for them.
   - ☐ Enjoy them–it's the "normal" people I avoid!
   - ☐ Other _____.

LEADER: Select a member of the group ahead of time to read aloud the Scripture passage. Then discuss the Questions for Interaction, dividing into subgroups of three to six.

We live in a world where many people with emotional problems are living out on the street. In Jesus' day, it wasn't much different. In the story today Jesus encounters a man possessed by a demon who showed some pretty bizarre behavior. We may not entirely understand the nature of the relationship between such demon possession and emotional illness, but one thing is clear—Jesus was able to miraculously heal the man, showing his power over every level of reality as well as over every illness. Read Mark 5:1-20, and note how the healed man responds.

The Healing of a Demon-possessed Man

5 Then they came to the other side of the sea, to the region of the Gerasenes. ²As soon as He got out of the boat, a man with an unclean spirit came out of the tombs and met Him. ³He lived in the tombs; and no one was able to restrain him any more—even with chains— ⁴because he often had been bound with shackles and chains, but had snapped off the chains and smashed the shackles. No one was strong enough to subdue him. ⁵And always, night and day, among the tombs and in the mountains, he was crying out and cutting himself with stones.

⁶When he saw Jesus from a distance, he ran and knelt down before Him. ⁷And he cried out with a loud voice, "What do You have to do with me, Jesus, Son of the Most High God? I beg You before God, don't torment me!" ⁸For He had told him, "Come out of the man, you unclean spirit!"

⁹"What is your name?" He asked him.

"My name is Legion," he answered Him, "because we are many." ¹⁰And he kept begging Him not to send them out of the region.

¹¹Now a large herd of pigs was there, feeding on the hillside. ¹²The demons begged Him, "Send us to the pigs, so we may enter them." ¹³And He gave them permission. Then the unclean spirits came out and entered the pigs, and the herd of about 2,000 rushed down the steep bank into the sea and drowned there. ¹⁴The men who tended them ran off and reported it in the town and the countryside, and people went to see what had happened. ¹⁵They came to Jesus and saw the man who had been demon-possessed by the legion sitting there, dressed and in his right mind; and they were afraid. ¹⁶The eyewitnesses described to them what had happened to the demon-possessed man and told about the pigs. ¹⁷Then they began to beg Him to leave their region.

¹⁸As He was getting into the boat, the man who had been demon-possessed kept begging Him to be with Him. ¹⁹But He would not let him; instead, He told him, "Go back home to your own people, and report to them how much the Lord has done for you and how He has had mercy on you." ²⁰So he went out and began to proclaim in the Decapolis how much Jesus had done for him; and they were all amazed.

Mark 5:1-20

QUESTIONS FOR INTERACTION

LEADER: Refer to the Summary and Study Notes at the end of this section as needed. If 30 minutes is not enough time to answer all of the questions in this section, conclude the Bible Study by answering questions 6 and 7.

1. If you lived in a small town where a man like this inhabited the cemetery, what would you do?
   - ❏ Have the police evict him.
   - ❏ Show him off to all my out-of-town friends when they visit.
   - ❏ Put him on the local football team—middle linebacker!
   - ❏ Steer clear of him.
   - ❏ Seek to get him some help.
   - ❏ Other _____.

2. Which of this man's symptoms, if any, seem to point to mental illness, and which ones, if any, seem to demand a more supernatural explanation?

3. What is the literal meaning, as well as the symbolic significance, of the name of the demons (see note on v. 9)?

4. Why do you think Jesus allowed the demons to enter the pigs?
   - ❏ It was a simple plea-bargain.
   - ❏ Pigs were thought of as worthless by Jews anyway.
   - ❏ It was a way of visualizing the fact that the demons had been cast out of the man.
   - ❏ Since he knew the pigs would drown, it was a convenient way of getting rid of them.
   - ❏ Other _____.

5. After the exorcism, why did the people of the town plead with Jesus to leave their region?

6. Does this story make you uncomfortable to think that demons can have such an effect on people? How does this affect how you think about Jesus' ability to help you with your problems?

7. Have you ever told your family and closest friends how much the Lord has done for you, like the healed man at the end of this story? If so, what happened? If not, what is preventing you?

GOING DEEPER: If your group has time and/or wants a challenge, go on to this question.

8. How does this story affect your attitudes and beliefs about demons and demon possession?

CARING TIME : APPLY THE LESSON AND PRAY FOR ONE ANOTHER | 15 MIN.

LEADER: Continue to encourage group members to invite new people to the group. Close the group prayer by thanking God for each member and for this time together.

Take some time now to encourage one another with a time of sharing and prayer. After responding to the following questions, share prayer requests and close with a group prayer.

1. Can you think of someone with severe problems that you should be supporting in prayer?

2. How would you like to thank God for deliverance from sin or evil in your life?

3. From what do you still need to be released? How can this group support you?

NEXT WEEK

This week we were reminded of the power that Jesus has over all evil as we saw him free a man from a legion of demons. We also saw how the grateful man spread the word about Jesus to all who would listen. In the coming week, ask the Holy Spirit to help you look at "strange" people in a new way and be open to God's will in helping these people where possible. Next week we will consider the experience of a woman who had been ill for twelve years, and who finally found healing from Jesus. We will see that there is always hope where Jesus is involved.

Summary: We now examine a second exorcism (see Session 2). This time Jesus confronts a man who is ravished by not one, but thousands of demons. This is the ultimate in possession. Once again Jesus demonstrates his power by casting out this combined force of demons and healing a man whose body and personality had been overwhelmed by their evil possession. This is the second of the four "power" stories by which the disciples come to understand that Jesus is no mere teacher.

5:1 they came to the other side of the sea. Jesus and his disciples were in a boat on the Sea of Galilee. This incident took place after Jesus calmed the fierce storm that threatened to swamp their boat (4:35–41). Given the fact that Jesus and the Twelve left the Capernaum side of the lake "when evening came" (4:35), by the time they arrived on the other side it was probably dark. **the region of the Gerasenes.** The precise location of their landing is not clear. However, it is on the other side of the lake from Capernaum, in Gentile territory, probably near the lower end of the lake.

5:2 He got out of the boat. No mention is made of the disciples in this story. Given what they had been through in the storm on the Sea of Galilee (4:35–41) and the fact that they landed in a Gentile region at night in a graveyard with a nightmare-like figure howling at them, it is not surprising that only Jesus seems to have gotten out of the boat to face this terror. **a man with an unclean spirit.** There was widespread belief that demons could enter and take control of a person's body, speaking and acting through that person. First-century people lived in dread of demons. Thus they avoided places like cemeteries, where demons were thought to dwell. The demons were understood to be Satan's legions. In overcoming them, Jesus was demonstrating his power over Satan and his work.

5:3–5 The picture painted of this man was that of a living terror: He was naked. Physically, he was so powerful he could not be subdued. He was cut up and perhaps bleeding, and he cried out in great distress living there among the tombs.

5:7 Son of the Most High God. The disciples asked in the previous story who Jesus is (4:41) and the demon-filled man, with supernatural insight, here points out his divine nature. Interestingly, this title is how God was often referred to by the Gentiles (Gen. 14:18–24; Dan. 4:17). **I beg You before God, don't torment me!** It is not clear what they feared. According to Jewish apocalyptic literature, the torment of demons was to take place at the time of the final judgment. Jesus' presence signals to them the beginning of the end times.

5:9 Legion. The name for a company consisting of 6,000 Roman soldiers. The man was occupied not by one but by a huge number of demons. Even in this ultimate of all evil situations, Jesus demonstrates his power over evil. It cannot stand against him even in its most virulent form.

5:10 Again, it is not clear what they feared. Perhaps they feared being banished to hell. Contrary to popular thought, hell is not the realm where Satan and his demons are in charge. The New Testament pictures it as the place of their torment. According to Jude 6, Christ would bind such disobedient spirits until the Day of Judgment. Nor is it clear that being allowed to enter the pigs–who were quickly drowned–was all that more desirable. The fact that they entered into pigs reveals their unclean, corrupt natures.

5:11 pigs. This was a Gentile herd. No Jew would raise pigs since they were considered unclean animals (Lev. 11:1–8). For a Jew to eat or touch a pig meant that he or she was defiled and thus unable to participate in worship until a ceremonial cleansing was performed.

5:13 rushed down the steep bank. The stampede of the herd gave evidence that the demons had, indeed, been driven out of the man. The pigs' mad suicidal rush to the sea shows what kind of creatures they are. Their destructive impact on the pigs is in sharp contrast to the peace and healing Jesus brought to the demoniac.

5:15 they were afraid. It might be expected that they would rejoice that this man who had terrorized them and whom they could no longer restrain was now healed. But instead they are fearful of Jesus, who has the power to overcome the demons and destroy their town herd.

5:19 In contrast to what Jesus said to the leper in 1:44, he wants this man to share the story of his healing. The difference is that the leper was Jewish and his story might cause people to realize that the Messiah had come before they knew what kind of Messiah he was to be. Gentiles, however, did not have such messianic expectations. Interestingly, what the ex-demoniac could tell them was limited. He could explain what he was like before he met Jesus, what had happened to him when he encountered Jesus, and what little he knew about Jesus. This first Gentile witness to Jesus had no theological training; he simply had an amazing story to tell by which God's nature would be revealed.

5:20 Decapolis. A league of 10 Gentile cities patterned after the Greek way of life. This is the first of several ventures by Jesus into Gentile areas, demonstrating what Mark later points out (13:10; 14:9), that the Gospel is to be preached to all nations.

SESSION 8 : A SICK WOMAN TOUCHES JESUS

SCRIPTURE MARK 5:24-34

LAST WEEK

In last week's session, we considered Jesus' miracle of freeing a man from a legion of demons. We saw the immediate change in this man's life and how he then shared with everyone he could what Jesus had done for him. This week we will look at another healing miracle–that of a woman who had been ill for 12 years, and no one had been able to help her. We will see that Jesus brings hope when all hope is gone.

ICE-BREAKER : CONNECT WITH YOUR GROUP | 15 MINUTES

LEADER: Open with a word of prayer, and be sure to welcome and introduce new group members. Choose one, two or all three of the Ice-Breaker questions.

Jesus frequently healed by touch, and the story we will look at shortly is one good example. But touch is somewhat ambivalent in our society–most people want to be touched, but some have a negative history with it. How about you? Share some of your own history with touch by answering the following questions.

1. What was the role of physical touch in your family?
   - ❏ We were a very "huggie" family.
   - ❏ We got "touched" alright–with the back of a hand!
   - ❏ Touching was the mom's department.
   - ❏ Touching was encroaching on someone else's space.
   - ❏ Touching was only done by the kids to irritate each other.
   - ❏ Nobody touched anybody.
   - ❏ Other _____.

2. Finish this sentence: "When I think of being held as a child, I think of ..."

3. Which of the following best expresses how you feel about physical touch today?

  ❏ "Four hugs a day keeps the doctor away."

  ❏ "Immediate family only."

  ❏ "A handshake is sufficient."

  ❏ "Keep your distance—good fences make good neighbors."

  ❏ Other _____.

BIBLE STUDY : READ SCRIPTURE AND DISCUSS | 30 MINUTES

LEADER: Select three members of the group ahead of time to read aloud the Scripture passage. Have one member read the part of Mark, the narrator; another read the part of Jesus; and another read the part of the woman. Then discuss the Questions for Interaction, dividing into subgroups of three to six.

In our country today we are accustomed to the best in medical care. Yet there are still times when the best that medical science has to offer just doesn't seem to be able to take care of the problem we have. In those times we can identify with the following story about a woman who had a problem with bleeding for 12 years. Just touching the hem of Jesus' garment healed her. We also can find healing from Jesus that we cannot find anywhere else. Read Mark 5:24–34, and note the role that faith again plays in this healing.

The Healing of a Sick Woman

Mark: [24]So Jesus went with him, and a large crowd was following and pressing against Him. [25]A woman suffering from bleeding for 12 years [26]had endured much under many doctors. She had spent everything she had, and was not helped at all. On the contrary, she became worse. [27]Having heard about Jesus, she came behind Him in the crowd and touched His robe. [28]For she said,

Woman: "If I can just touch His robes, I'll be made well!"

Mark: [29]Instantly her flow of blood ceased, and she sensed in her body that she was cured of her affliction. [30]At once Jesus realized in Himself that power had gone out from Him. He turned around in the crowd and said,

Jesus: "Who touched My robes?"

Mark: [31]His disciples said to Him, "You see the crowd pressing against You, and You say, 'Who touched Me?' "

Mark: ³²So He was looking around to see who had done this. ³³Then the woman, knowing what had happened to her, came with fear and trembling, fell down before Him, and told Him the whole truth.

Jesus: ³⁴"Daughter," He said to her, "your faith has made you well. Go in peace and be free from your affliction."

Mark 5:24–34

QUESTIONS FOR INTERACTION

LEADER: Refer to the Summary and Study Notes at the end of this section as needed. If 30 minutes is not enough time to answer all of the questions in this section, conclude the Bible Study by answering questions 6 and 7.

1. When it comes to seeking help when you need it, how assertive are you likely to be?
   - ❑ I'll suffer silently–I don't want to bother anybody.
   - ❑ Well, if the pain gets too great and other people aren't too busy, I might say something.
   - ❑ I can take care of myself, I don't need help.
   - ❑ When I need help, I know how to say so.
   - ❑ When I need help, I make sure the whole world knows it.
   - ❑ Other _____.

2. Why might this woman have been so subtle in the way she reached out to Jesus for help?
   - ❑ She was shy.
   - ❑ She didn't want to be disappointed in public.
   - ❑ She was ceremonially "unclean" and knew she shouldn't be there.
   - ❑ Other _____.

3. Put yourself in this woman's place. What thoughts might be racing through your mind as:
   - ❑ You reach out toward Jesus' robe to touch it?
   - ❑ You feel healing in your body?
   - ❑ Jesus suddenly stops and asks "Who touched My robe?"

4. The woman was instantly healed. Why was it still important to Jesus that the person who touched him be identified?

5. What insights can you gain from Jesus' response to the woman in verse 34?

6. When do you remember being the most desperate for God's help? How did you "reach out" to Jesus?

7. Where are you right now in terms of this story?
- ❏ Just rushing through the crowds without feeling anyone's touch.
- ❏ Trying all the "doctors" and getting nowhere.
- ❏ Deciding to try Jesus, but afraid to hope.
- ❏ Feeling Jesus' healing within me.
- ❏ Trying to run away unnoticed.
- ❏ Ready to declare what Jesus did for me.
- ❏ Other _____.

GOING DEEPER: If your group has time and/or wants a challenge, go on to this question.

8. Why was this woman healed when nobody else in the crowd was healed? Is this favoritism on Jesus' part, or are other factors involved?

CARING TIME : APPLY THE LESSON AND PRAY FOR ONE ANOTHER | 15 MIN.

LEADER: Remember to start talking with your group about their mission—perhaps by sharing the vision of multiplying into two groups by the end of this study of Jesus' miracles.

Gather around each other now for a time of sharing and prayer, remembering the hope that Jesus brings to every situation in your life.

1. How was your walk with the Lord this past week?

2. What false ways have "bled you dry" in the past? Take time to thank God in prayer for the ways he has helped you when others could not.

3. What kind of healing do you need from Jesus right now? Pray for his touch in your life.

NEXT WEEK

This week we considered the experience of a woman who had been ill for 12 years, and who finally found healing and hope in Jesus. We were reminded that with God nothing is impossible. In the coming week, pray for and encourage someone you know who is dealing with a long-term difficult situation. Next week we will look at a well-known miracle where Jesus walked on water during a storm, and we will see what it teaches us about Jesus' presence in the storms of our lives.

Summary: This is the third of the four "power" stories Mark uses to empha- size Jesus' absolute and universal authority over all forces that oppress humani- ty. Just as the Gentile demoniac would have been considered "unclean" by the Jews, so this woman with the interminable menstrual flow would be viewed as an "unclean" person to be avoided by those who wished to maintain their purity before God.

5:25 A woman. While on the way to Jairus' home to see his dying daughter, this woman, part of the crowd following after Jesus to see what he could do for Jairus' daugh- ter, approached him in secret. She should not have been there in the crowd. Because of the nature of her illness she was considered "unclean." If people touched her, they too would become "unclean" and be rendered unable to participate in ceremonial worship until they went through a prescribed cleansing ritual. **suffering from bleeding.** This was probably a steady hemorrhaging from her womb. Not only would this lead to obvious physical and emo- tional problems, but such bleeding rendered her ritually impure (Lev. 15:25-33). She was cut off from involvement in the religious life of her people, such as worshiping in the temple, and she would have been prohibited from having sexual relations with her husband. Since many people assumed that chronic problems like this were God's judgment upon a person for their sin, she undoubtedly experienced some measure of condemnation from others as well. All of this may have contributed to the surreptitious way she approached Jesus.

5:26 endured much under many doctors. Mark mentioning that the woman was not helped at all, though she had gone to many doctors, was not casting aspersions on doctors, but highlighting the seriousness of the woman's condition.

5:29 Instantly. This is a prominent word throughout Mark's gospel. It emphasizes the irresistible power inherent in Jesus' person. The same word is translated in verse 30 as "At once." This was a real miracle. Then and there she was healed, and she knew it.

5:30 power. This is the creative, healing power of God. The implication is not that Jesus had a limited supply of divine energy that was somehow drained by this event, but that he was the agent through whom God's power was transmitted to the woman. **Who touched My robes?** Jesus desired a relationship with those he helped. He was not an impersonal power source.

5:31 You see the crowd pressing against You, and You say, 'Who touched Me?' As in 4:38, the disciples fail to understand Jesus or what he is about. They can only see that his stopping to ask what seems to be a foolish question is wasting the limited time they have to get to Jairus' house before his daughter dies. In the press of the crowd undoubtedly many people were touching him, yet Jesus was aware that a special work had been done for one person and he desired to know who that was.

5:32 He was looking around. Jesus insists that the person who touched him identify herself. At first glance this seems cruel since Jesus forces this woman—who should not have been there in the first place and who had a disease she probably would not have wanted to talk about publicly—to identify herself. However, her healing will not be complete without this, since her illness had not only physical but emotional and social consequences. In the same way that he insisted that the leper go through the cleansing ritual and thus be admitted back into society (1:44), here Jesus makes it publicly known that she has been healed so that she can once again have a normal religious and relational life.

5:33 with fear and trembling. Fear is a common element in all these four power stories (4:40–41; 5:15; 5:36). Not only do people in the scenes face frightening circumstances, but there is fear before Jesus as well. Everyone is caught off guard by his authority that exceeds all their expectations. This woman may have feared that she had done something wrong; she may have feared that Jesus would shame her in front of everyone; she may have feared that her healing would be revoked.

5:34 Daughter. This word changes everything. It stresses that she is indeed a child of God, loved and not under his judgment. It affirms that she is no longer a social outcast, but is in community with the other children of God. **your faith has made you well.** It was her faith that impelled her to reach out to Jesus—the source of healing power. The word Jesus uses to tell her that she is healed comes from the same root as the words "salvation" and "Savior." Spiritual as well as physical healing is in view here. **Go in peace.** Jesus did not mean by this, "Be free from worry." This phrase means "Be complete, be whole." Although each of these four incidents portrays an extreme situation in which there is no hope humanly speaking, each ends in peace as the result of the power of Jesus (4:39; 5:15,34,42).

SESSION 9 : JESUS WALKS ON WATER

SCRIPTURE MATTHEW 14:22—36

LAST WEEK

Last week we discovered how a woman who could find healing nowhere else, found it in Jesus' touch. We were reminded that Jesus can bring hope into any situation, if we just have faith in his love and power. This week we will consider one of Jesus' most famous miracles—that of walking on water during a storm. We will see what it teaches us about Jesus' presence in the storms of our lives.

ICE-BREAKER : CONNECT WITH YOUR GROUP | 15 MINUTES

LEADER: Open with a word of prayer. Welcome and introduce new group members. Choose one, two or all three Ice-Breaker questions, depending on your group's needs.

The disciples were "terrified" in today's Scripture passage when they thought they saw a ghost walking on the water. Take turns sharing about experiences you've had with being frightened.

1. What is the scariest movie or news report you have ever seen?

2. Why are people more afraid after dark?

3. How did you react as a child when you saw or heard something a little creepy or hard to explain?
   - ❏ I called for my parents.
   - ❏ I was always the one to get up and check it out.
   - ❏ I hid under the covers.
   - ❏ I cried.
   - ❏ I acted brave.
   - ❏ I tried to scare my little brother or sister.
   - ❏ Other _____.

LEADER: Select a member of the group ahead of time to read aloud the Scripture passage. Then discuss the Questions for Interaction, dividing into subgroups of three to six.

Jesus' miracles included not only healings, but also times when he was able to demonstrate his power over the whole natural world. Such was the case when he walked on the stormy waters of the Sea of Galilee. Read Matthew 14:22-36, and note Peter's response to Jesus.

Jesus Walks on the Water

[22]Immediately He made the disciples get into the boat and go ahead of Him to the other side, while He dismissed the crowds. [23]After dismissing the crowds, He went up on the mountain by Himself to pray. When evening came, He was there alone. [24]But the boat was already over a mile from land, battered by the waves, because the wind was against them. [25]Around three in the morning, He came toward them walking on the sea. [26]When the disciples saw Him walking on the sea, they were terrified. "It's a ghost!" they said, and cried out in fear.

[27]Immediately Jesus spoke to them. "Have courage! It is I. Don't be afraid."

[28]"Lord, if it's You," Peter answered Him, "command me to come to You on the water."

[29]"Come!" He said.

And climbing out of the boat, Peter started walking on the water and came toward Jesus. [30]But when he saw the strength of the wind, he was afraid. And beginning to sink he cried out, "Lord, save me!"

[31]Immediately Jesus reached out His hand, caught hold of him, and said to him, "You of little faith, why did you doubt?" [32]When they got into the boat, the wind ceased. [33]Then those in the boat worshiped Him and said, "Truly You are the Son of God!"

[34]Once they crossed over, they came to land at Gennesaret. [35]When the men of that place recognized Him, they alerted the whole vicinity and brought to Him all who were sick. [36]They were begging Him that they might only touch the tassel on His robe. And as many as touched it were made perfectly well.

Matthew 14:22-36

QUESTIONS FOR INTERACTION

LEADER: Refer to the Summary and Study Notes at the end of this section as needed. If 30 minutes is not enough time to answer all of the questions in this section, conclude the Bible Study by answering question 7.

1. When do you last remember seeing something so strange that you didn't believe what you saw?

2. In this story, what makes the disciples think they are seeing a ghost? How do they react to this apparition?

3. What does Jesus' ability to walk on water say about his nature (Job 9:8; Ps. 77:16–19)?

4. Why do you think Peter wanted to walk on water also?

5. What did Peter do wrong?
   - ❑ He stepped out of the boat in the first place.
   - ❑ He took his eyes off Jesus and focused on the dangers instead.
   - ❑ He cried for help when he should have just trusted.
   - ❑ Other _____.

6. When have you, like Peter, taken a risk based on your faith in Jesus? How does Peter's experience contribute to your understanding of what happened with you?

7. Where do you feel that God is calling you to "get out of the boat" today?
   - ❑ In my relationships–taking more risks with people.
   - ❑ In my future planning–doing something I have been afraid to try.
   - ❑ In my inner life–facing an inner storm.
   - ❑ In my spiritual walk–trusting God to hold me up.
   - ❑ Other _____.

GOING DEEPER: If your group has time and/or wants a challenge, go on to this question.

8. Is it possible for a human being to jump into the storms of life with absolutely no doubts? If so, how does one reach that level of faith? If not, when is a little doubt normal, and when does it become disabling?

CARING TIME : APPLY THE LESSON AND PRAY FOR ONE ANOTHER | 15 MIN.

LEADER: Have you identified someone in the group that could be a leader for a new small group when your group divides? How could you encourage and mentor that person?

For us to be able to have faith in the storms of life we need more than study—we need support and encouragement. This is your time to give that to each other. Share your responses to the following questions before closing in prayer.

1. What do you look forward to most about these meetings?

2. Where do you feel as if you are stepping out into a "storm" right now? How can this group support you in prayer concerning this "storm"?

3. How can this group pray for you in relation to where God is calling you to "get out of the boat" (question 7)?

NEXT WEEK

Today we considered the amazing miracle of Jesus walking on the water. We also gave some thought to what it means to "step out of the boat" as Peter did, and follow through in faith. In the coming week, ask the Holy Spirit to help you to step out of your comfort zone and follow God's will, wherever that may lead. Next week we will look at Jesus' healing of people's blindness and what it might mean for our own areas of "blindness."

Summary: Matthew, Mark and John all follow the story of the feeding of the five thousand with this scene. (Luke omits it.) This walking on water demonstrates Jesus' power over nature itself. What surprises us at first in this story is that the power is extended to another person–Peter. And yet Jesus elsewhere declared "The one who believes in Me will also do the works that I do. And he will do even greater things than these, because I am going to the Father" (John 14:12). Thus, an important part of what Jesus does for us is to grant us the power to act in his name, sometimes even to the point of doing the seemingly impossible.

14:23 After dismissing the crowds. While neither Matthew nor Mark accounts for the abrupt departure of Jesus from the crowd, the reason is given in John 6:14-15. Apparently the crowd, sensing that the feeding of the five thousand was a sign that Jesus was indeed the messianic prophet for whom they had long been waiting, tried in its enthusiasm to make Jesus their king. The disciples are sent away, perhaps, to keep them from harm in the face of this zealous crowd, or perhaps to keep them catching this false messianic fever. **He went ... to pray.** In the midst of great success and popular acclaim, once again Jesus goes off to pray.

14:24 the wind was against them. Once again, as in their slow trip across the lake earlier (Mark 4:37), the elements work against the disciples.

14:25 three in the morning. Literally, "the fourth watch." This was the way the Roman soldiers marked time. The fourth watch ran from 3 to 6 A.M. Assuming the disciples set out to sea in the late afternoon, they had been struggling at the oars for probably seven or more hours. **walking on the sea.** While it has already been established that Jesus is Lord over the wind and the water (Mark 4: 39,41), this is another new action that went well beyond the expectations of the disciples.

14:26 terrified. Once before on this lake they were terrified by an event they did not expect and did not understand, namely the calming of the sea by Jesus (Mark 4:41). This is the terror of experiencing something that defies all categories of understanding. **a ghost.** The sea, especially at night, was thought to be a dwelling place for demons. The disciples had no idea of what horror might await them as this apparition approached.

14:27 Have courage! It is I. Don't be afraid. This is the language of God. The call to have courage because of God's presence with his people is a common theme in the Old Testament prophets (Isa. 41:10; 43:5; Jer. 1:8). **It is I.** Literally, "I am." This phrase can just be a simple declaration by Jesus that there is no ghost to be afraid of. However, in the Old Testament this is a phrase used by God to describe himself (Ex. 3:1-14 where in the burning bush God reveals himself to Moses by this name). This phrase reveals that Jesus is not just a new Moses or another king in the line of David. He is also the Son of God. Since the Old Testament often refers to God as the one who treads on water (Job 9:8; 38:16; Ps. 77:19; Isa. 43:2,16), it is clear that this miracle was intended as a sign of Jesus' divine identity.

14:28 Peter's action demonstrates what faith is all about: it is acting with confidence in Jesus even when circumstances seem to be impossible. It is not a foolhardiness based on personal bravado, but trust in the character of Jesus to protect and guide his people.

14:30 At first it appears Peter was successful in this incredible act. However, the frightening uncertainty of the situation coupled with the power of the wind and waves beating against him led him to doubt Jesus' word: thus, he faltered. **Lord, save me!** Peter's cry sums up the cry of all those who find themselves in desperate situations: his hope is solely in Jesus to rescue him from the danger of the sea. Likewise, all disciples are to call upon Jesus to rescue them from the danger of sin.

14:31 You of little faith. The problem Peter faced was not the circumstances, but inadequate trust in Jesus despite the circumstances. He has not yet fully come to trust in the power and the person of Jesus.

14:33 Truly You are the Son of God! It is unclear how fully the disciples grasped the full truth of what they were saying. In the Old Testament, the term "Son of God" was used to describe God's appointed king who was to reign over Israel in God's stead (Ps. 2:7). Did the disciples think of Jesus merely in this sense? It is unlikely that any of them fully appreciated what it meant that Jesus was God's Son until after his death and resurrection.

14:36 the tassel on His robe. This recalls the healing of the woman in Mark 5:25–28. Jesus was so powerful that even touching the very edge of his garment, i.e., making the most minimal contact with him, was sufficient to experience that power.

SESSION 10 : TWO BLIND PEOPLE HEALED

SCRIPTURE MARK 8:22–26; 10:46–52

LAST WEEK

In last week's session, we saw Jesus once again show his power over nature as he walked on the water during a storm. We were reminded that sometimes we need to "step out of the boat" as Peter did, and keep our eyes on Jesus, trusting him to guide us through every difficult situation we may face. This week we will look at Jesus' healing of two people with blindness, and we will consider how this relates to our own spiritual "blindness."

ICE-BREAKER : CONNECT WITH YOUR GROUP | 15 MINUTES

LEADER: Choose one or two of the Ice-Breaker questions. If you have a new group member, you may want to do all three. Remember to stick closely to the three-part agenda and the time allowed for each segment.

Most of us are not blind–at least not in the physical sense. However, we all can be "blind" to some things at one time or another. When has this been true for you? Share something about yourself by answering the following questions.

1. When you were in high school, which of the following were you most "blind" to?
   - ❑ Anything good about my parents.
   - ❑ Anything bad about my parents.
   - ❑ My own abilities.
   - ❑ Flaws in my girlfriend or boyfriend.
   - ❑ The injustices of the world.
   - ❑ Anything beyond what my friends were doing.
   - ❑ Anything having to do with religion.
   - ❑ Other _____.

2. What was the most dramatic "eye-opening" event you have experienced in your life? How did it happen?

3. If you completely lost your sight, what would you miss seeing the most?

LEADER: Select two
members of the group
ahead of time to read
aloud the Scripture
passage. Have one
person read 8:22–26,
and the other read
10:46–52. Then dis-
cuss the Questions for
Interaction, dividing
into subgroups of
three to six.

When John the Baptist began to question whether Jesus was indeed the Christ, one of the signs that Jesus pointed to as evidence of his identity was that "the blind receive their sight" (Matt. 11:5). Indeed, healing the blind was an oft-repeated miracle for Jesus. We are all blind in some sense to the spiritual world, and even to the miracles of God in this world, so we all need to have our eyes opened. Read Mark 8:22–26; 10:46–52, and note how these miracles of healing the blind are, in a sense, our own story.

Two Blind People Healed

Reader One: ²²Then they came to Bethsaida. They brought a blind man to Him and begged Him to touch him. ²³He took the blind man by the hand and brought him out of the village. Spitting on his eyes and laying His hands on him, He asked him, "Do you see anything?"

²⁴He looked up and said, "I see people—they look to me like trees walking."

²⁵Again He placed His hands on his eyes, and he saw distinctly. He was cured and could see everything clearly. ²⁶Then He sent him home, saying, "Don't even go into the village."

Reader Two: ⁴⁶They came to Jericho. And as He was leaving Jericho with His disciples and a large crowd, Bartimaeus (the son of Timaeus), a blind beggar, was sitting by the road. ⁴⁷When he heard that it was Jesus the Nazarene, he began to cry out, "Son of David, Jesus, have mercy on me!" ⁴⁸Many people told him to keep quiet, but he was crying out all the more, "Have mercy on me, Son of David!" ⁴⁹Jesus stopped and said, "Call him."

So they called the blind man and said to him, "Have courage! Get up; He's calling for you." ⁵⁰He threw off his coat, jumped up, and came to Jesus.

⁵¹Then Jesus answered him, "What do you want Me to do for you?"

"*Rabbouni,*" the blind man told Him, "I want to see!"

⁵²"Go your way," Jesus told him. "Your faith has healed you." Immediately he could see and began to follow Him on the road.

Mark 8:22–26; 10:46–52

LEADER: Refer to the Summary and Study Notes at the end of this section as needed. If 30 minutes is not enough time to answer all of the questions in this section, conclude the Bible Study by answering questions 6 and 7.

1. With which of these two blind men do you most identify, and why?
   - ❑ The man of Bethsaida–because I've come to Christ in stages.
   - ❑ The man of Bethsaida–because I never seem to "get it" the first time.
   - ❑ Bartimaeus–because people want to keep me from getting better.
   - ❑ Bartimaeus–because nobody can keep me quiet when it comes to Jesus.
   - ❑ Bartimaeus–because I just follow Jesus along the road of my life.
   - ❑ Other _____.

2. In what ways does the limited healing of the blind man in 8:24 prepare the way for how the disciples perceive Jesus when he asked them, "Who do people say that I am?" and "Who do you say that I am?" (8:27–33)? In what way is their spiritual sight partial, and when is their sight clarified?

3. The story of Bartimaeus immediately follows the story of how James and John maneuvered to get the chief places in Jesus' kingdom (10:35–45). How do Bartimaeus' words and deeds serve as an example, even to the Twelve?

4. The first story is the final miracle before Peter's climactic confession that Jesus is the Christ (8:29). The second story is the final miracle Jesus performs before entering Jerusalem to be crucified. What might be Mark's point in placing these two miracles of sight just prior to two major events in Jesus' ministry?

5. Why do you think Jesus asked Bartimaeus, who was obviously blind, "What do you want Me to do for you?"
   - ❑ He thought Bartimaeus might have something else wrong in addition to blindness.
   - ❑ He wanted Bartimaeus to decide whether he wanted to get better or keep this social "crutch."
   - ❑ He wanted Bartimaeus to voice faith in him to heal him.
   - ❑ He just wanted Bartimaeus to feel that he was in control of his own life and healing.
   - ❑ Other _____.

6. In the first story, the blind man sees clearly only in stages, and in the second story he sees clearly immediately. In your own coming to Christ, what did you see immediately, and what have you been able to see only over the course of time?

7. Were Jesus to come to you right now and ask, "What do you want Me to do for you?" how would you respond?

If your group has time and/or wants a challenge, go on to this question.

8. In what way do even Christians sometimes see people as things ("like trees walking")? How can a "second touch" from Christ help us to see people as people?

CARING TIME : APPLY THE LESSON AND PRAY FOR ONE ANOTHER | 15 MIN.

LEADER: Be sure that everyone is receiving prayer support during this important time. Continue to pray that the empty chair will be filled.

Gather around each other now in this Caring Time, and pray that Christ would help each of you to see and understand his love and the sacrifice he made for your salvation. Begin by sharing your responses to the following questions. Then take some time to share prayer requests and pray for one another.

1. What aspect of your Christian faith would you like to be able to see and understand in a more complete way?

2. Pray that group members will be able to see the needs of the people in their lives more clearly.

3. How can this group support you in prayer in relation to how you answered question 7?

NEXT WEEK

This week we considered two different cases of Jesus healing the blind. In one case the healing was gradual, and in the other it was instantaneous. We were reminded that we all need to be healed from spiritual blindness, and this healing may occur differently for each person. In the coming week, let Jesus heal someone through your words and deeds. Next week we will look at the raising of Lazarus from the dead, and how his story can help us face death and the fear of death.

Summary: Previous to this, Jesus had just admonished the Twelve for their spiritual blindness and deafness (8:17-18). While both of these stories involve the healing of a blind man, the point of each story is quite different. The first story accented the blindness of the disciples in terms of understanding who Jesus is. The second story accents the identity of Jesus as the Messianic Son of David come to free those who trust him. Happening just prior to Jesus' final entry into Jerusalem, it is a demonstration of faith that stands in stark contrast to the determined resistance and opposition Jesus will soon face. This story may also be intended as a reminder of the earlier one in that it follows a scene where the disciples have again demonstrated that they really do not understand the nature of Jesus and his kingdom (10:35-45). They are still blind or, at best, have only partial sight.

8:22 Bethsaida. This was a town at the mouth of the Jordan River on the shore of the Sea of Galilee.

8:23 brought him out of the village. Perhaps Jesus wanted this blind man to get away from the social context in which people treated him like a dependent child. He had to go where people weren't use to treating him like a blind man. He had to go where people didn't do to him what the crowd did to Bartimaeus (next story)—trying to keep him as the dependent creature he used to be. This may be why Jesus later specifically tells him not to go back into the village where he had once been a beggar (v. 26). Note that Jesus sent him "home," so evidently "home" was not in the village. **Spitting on his eyes and laying His hands on him.** Since most of Jesus' miracles were accomplished simply by a word, it is unclear why this was necessary. Since such actions were involved in other healing practices, it may be that Jesus used this means as a way to encourage the faith of the blind man.

8:24 they look to me like trees walking. The man's sight is improved, but not enough so he could function as a person whose vision is good. He probably once had his sight, since he knows what a tree looks like.

8:25 Again. This is the only healing that requires a second touch on the part of Jesus. Mark's placement of this story right after the disciples' incomprehension of the meaning of the feeding miracles, and just prior to their confession of faith in Jesus as the Messiah, may indicate he is using this story to illustrate how difficult it was for the disciples to grasp Jesus' identity.

10:46 Jericho. Jericho is a city about 18 miles east of Jerusalem and the place where travelers recrossed the Jordan back into Israel. It was the site of Herod's magnificent winter place and the home of many of the priests that served in the temple in Jerusalem. **a large crowd.** These were pilgrims on their way to Jerusalem for the Passover Feast. Every male over 12 years of age living within a 15 mile radius of Jerusalem was expected to attend. Many Jews from throughout the Roman Empire and the East would likewise try to visit Jerusalem during Passover.

10:47 Son of David, Jesus. This is the only time in Mark's gospel that this title is used of Jesus, although Matthew and Luke use it quite often. At the time of Jesus it was some-times used as a title of respect for someone perceived to be particularly blessed by God. However, its occurrence at this point in the narrative (just prior to Jesus' death) indicates Mark wanted it to be understood as a messianic title. While Jesus told the man in chapter eight not to tell what had happened, here Jesus lets the statement of Bartimaeus stand. He accepts the title. The time for secrecy is past. From now on he would be recognized as the messianic King.

10:48 Many people told him to keep quiet. We don't know why the crowd reacted in this way. People may have assumed that he was too insignificant to be bothered with by a man as great as Jesus. Or, like many today, they may have become impatient with the demands of the poor and disabled, and simply thought he should be quietly accepting his fate. The crowd had no stake in Bartimaeus getting better. **he was crying out all the more.** His faith had latched on to Jesus and he would not be deterred.

10:50 He threw off his coat. This would have been his garment that was probably laid in front of him, and upon which he gathered alms. His casting it aside so that it would not get in his way of getting to Jesus indicates his single-minded determination. If he was not healed, there would be no guarantee that he, a blind man, would find it again. The coins he had collected upon it would be scattered among the crowd and lost. This is a picture of someone forsaking all to come after Jesus (8:34).

10:51 What do you want Me to do for you? Although his need was obvious, the fact that he must declare it shows his conviction that Jesus can heal him.

10:52 Your faith has healed you. This healing was not a matter of impersonal power, but of a relationship of faith in One who is compassionate and gracious (2:5; 5:34). **began to follow Him on the road.** His healing freed him to become a disciple. Likewise, as the Twelve become fully aware of Jesus' nature and mission, they too will be expected to follow in his way.

SESSION 11 : LAZARUS IS RAISED

SCRIPTURE JOHN 11:1-3,17-27,38-47

LAST WEEK

Jesus' healing of two blind people was our focus in last week's session. We were reminded how we all need to be healed of spiritual "blindness." We also discussed how we should keep our eyes open to the needs of the people around us. This week we will focus on the raising of Lazarus from the dead, and see what this story says to us about our own spiritual journey and how we will face death.

ICE-BREAKER : CONNECT WITH YOUR GROUP | 15 MINUTES

LEADER:Open with a word of prayer. Choose one, two or all three Ice-Breaker questions, depending on your group's needs.

Nothing is more certain in life than the fact that we will have to encounter death. For many of us, this experience first occurs when we are young. Take turns sharing some of your own history with death and mourning.

1. What death most affected you when you were a child or adolescent? Was it the death of a family member, friend or pet? How did you react at the time?

2. When was the last time you attended a funeral? What happened that seemed to strengthen those in mourning? What did you notice that you thought might not have been helpful?

3. When you cry, what are you most likely to cry about?
   - ☐ A sad movie.
   - ☐ A sad memory.
   - ☐ A beautiful gesture by a loved one.
   - ☐ Smashing your thumb with a hammer.
   - ☐ Other _____.

LEADER: Select three members of the group ahead of time to read aloud the Scripture passage. Have one member read the part of John, the narrator; another read the part of Martha; and the third person the part of Jesus. Then discuss the Questions for Interaction, dividing into subgroups of three to six.

Jesus' own resurrection is not the only one spoken of in Scripture or even the New Testament. Here Jesus raises Lazarus from the dead, in a kind of fore-shadowing of his own resurrection. Lazarus was the brother of Mary and Martha, two of Jesus' most faithful followers. Word is sent to Jesus that Lazarus is ill, but Jesus delays in returning, and in the interim, Lazarus dies. Read John 11:1–3,17–27,38–47, and note how Jesus related to the ones who mourned Lazarus.

Jesus Raises Lazarus from the Dead

John: **11** Now a man was sick, Lazarus, from Bethany, the village of Mary and her sister Martha. [2]Mary was the one who anointed the Lord with fragrant oil and wiped His feet with her hair, and it was her brother Lazarus who was sick. [3]So the sisters sent a message to Him: "Lord, the one You love is sick." ... [17]When Jesus arrived, He found that Lazarus had already been in the tomb four days. [18]Bethany was near Jerusalem (about two miles away). [19]Many of the Jews had come to Martha and Mary to comfort them about their brother. [20]As soon as Martha heard that Jesus was coming, she went to meet Him. But Mary remained seated in the house. [21]Then Martha said to Jesus,

Martha: "Lord, if You had been here, my brother wouldn't have died. [22]Yet even now I know that whatever You ask from God, God will give You."

Jesus: [23]"Your brother will rise again," Jesus told her.

Martha: [24]Martha said, "I know that he will rise again in the resurrection at the last day."

Jesus: [25]Jesus said to her, "I am the resurrection and the life. The one who believes in Me, even if he dies, will live. [26]Everyone who lives and believes in Me will never die—ever. Do you believe this?"

Martha: [27]"Yes, Lord," she told Him, "I believe You are the Messiah, the Son of God, who was to come into the world." ...

Jesus: [38]Then Jesus, angry in Himself again, came to the tomb. It was a cave, and a stone was lying against it. [39]"Remove the stone," Jesus said.

Martha: Martha, the dead man's sister, told Him, "Lord, he already stinks. It's been four days."

Jesus:	⁴⁰Jesus said to her, "Didn't I tell you that if you believed you would see the glory of God?" ⁴¹So they removed the stone. Then Jesus raised His eyes and said, "Father, I thank You that You heard Me. ⁴²I know that You always hear Me, but because of the crowd standing here I said this, so they may believe You sent Me." ⁴³After He said this, He shouted with a loud voice, "Lazarus, come out!"
John:	⁴⁴The dead man came out bound hand and foot with linen strips and with his face wrapped in a cloth. Jesus said to them,
Jesus:	"Loose him and let him go."
John:	⁴⁵Therefore many of the Jews who came to Mary and saw what He did believed in Him. ⁴⁶But some of them went to the Pharisees and told them what Jesus had done. ⁴⁷So the chief priests and the Pharisees convened the Sanhedrin and said, "What are we going to do since this man does many signs?

John 11:1–3,17–27,38–47

QUESTIONS FOR INTERACTION

LEADER: Refer to the Summary and Study Notes at the end of this section as needed. If 30 minutes is not enough time to answer all of the questions in this section, conclude the Bible Study by answering questions 6 and 7.

1. If you or someone in your immediate family were seriously ill, who would be the first person you would call, and what would you expect them to do to be supportive?

2. When Martha goes out to see Jesus, why do you think Mary stays home?
   □ She's irritated with Jesus for not coming earlier.
   □ She just wants to be alone for a while.
   □ She's tired.
   □ Other _____.

3. What do you think Martha was feeling when she said, "Lord, if You had been here, my brother wouldn't have died" (v. 21)?

4. If Martha had faith in Jesus (v. 22), why was she hesitant when Jesus asked for the stone to be removed from the entrance to the tomb (v. 39)?

5. What was the purpose of the prayer that Jesus said just before calling Lazarus forth from the tomb (vv. 41–42)?

6. Where is your spiritual life right now in the terms of this story?

7. What promise of God do you need to believe more fully in order to "see the glory of God"?

GOING DEEPER: If your group has time and/or wants a challenge, go on to this question.

8. Both sisters made the statement that if Jesus had been with them Lazarus would not have died. Is it always true that if Jesus is truly with us, bad things won't happen? What can we expect of Jesus when he is truly with us?

CARING TIME : APPLY THE LESSON AND PRAY FOR ONE ANOTHER | 15 MIN.

LEADER: Conclude the prayer time today by asking for God's guidance in determining the future mission and outreach of this group.

Remembering how Jesus mourned with those who mourned Lazarus, come to him now with all of your joys and sorrows. After responding to the following questions, share prayer requests and close with a group prayer.

1. How has Jesus been at work in your life this past week? How do you need his guidance and wisdom in the coming week?

2. What has recently "come back to life" for you–a relationship, a hope for the future, your faith, etc.–that you would like to thank God for?

3. How can this group pray for you in relation to the next step in your spiritual journey (see question 6)?

NEXT WEEK

Today we considered the resurrection of Lazarus from the tomb, and what it says to us about our own spiritual journey. We were reminded that Jesus offers life-giving grace now and eternal life in the future. In the coming week, comfort and encourage someone who is going through a time of grief or loss. Next week we will focus on a miracle that Jesus did to a fig tree and how it illustrates our need to live a fruitful life.

Summary: The greatest test of any religious faith is what it says to us when we face the reality of death. Lazarus, brother of Mary and Martha, becomes seriously ill and the sisters send for Jesus. He delays in coming, however, and Lazarus dies. What will this mean for the faith of Mary and Martha? Will they turn from him in anger and resentment? Although their faith seems to be strained at first, Jesus' gentle affirmations of his power over death reassure them, and when he performs the incredible act of raising Lazarus from the grave, they begin to see the full implications of who Jesus is. The resurrection of Lazarus prepares them for the even more significant resurrection to come—Jesus' own resurrection, a resurrection that paves the way for all who have faith in him to have victory over death itself.

11:2 Mary ... who anointed the Lord with fragrant oil. Apparently John, aware that the story of Jesus' anointing was a familiar one to his readers (Mark 14:1–11), used this incident to identify Mary even though it doesn't occur in this gospel until chapter 12.

11:3 the one You love. Jesus was a friend to Lazarus and his sisters (Luke 10:38–42). Not only do the sisters remark on the love Jesus had for Lazarus, but so do the villagers when they see that Jesus is moved to tears at the tomb of Lazarus (11:33–36).

11:18 about two miles away. This proximity meant that the story of Lazarus being raised to life reached the authorities in Jerusalem quickly. Jesus seemed to use Bethany as a base of operation while he was in Jerusalem (Matt. 21:17).

11:21 if You had been here. Since Lazarus had died probably even before Jesus received the message (11:1–7), and since Martha also adds a statement of trust in Christ's power to do something wonderful "even now" (v. 22), this is not a rebuke but an expression of regret. It implies that if Jesus had been on the scene before his death, Lazarus could have been saved.

11:22 Yet even now I know. Given her confusion in verse 39, this may not be an expectation of the miracle that does in fact occur. But it is at least an expression of a faith that Christ is in control, and will bring about what is best even now.

11:23 will rise again. The Pharisees and other Jewish groups believed in a general resurrection. Martha would have understood Jesus' comment as simply an appropriate expression of comfort at a funeral. Other mourners, wishing to comfort her and assure her that they knew Lazarus had been a good man, probably said very similar things to her.

11:25 I am the resurrection and the life. This claim would jar anyone at a funeral. By it, Jesus focuses Martha's attention, not on the doctrine of the general resurrection, but on him as the source of that resurrection (5:24–29). **even if he dies, will live.** Spiritual life that will not end by physical death is in view here. In this verse and in verse 26, Jesus is asserting his sovereign power over death and his ability to "the Son gives life to whomever He wishes" (5:21).

11:26 Do you believe this? Jesus directly confronts Martha with his claim. Does she see him only as a healer or as the Lord of life? Jesus on several occasions made a point of giving his followers an opportunity to declare where they stood in relationship to him. A similar instance is when he asked Peter, "But you? … who do you say that I am?" (Matt. 16:15).

11:27 In this verse, Martha declares by means of four terms exactly who Jesus is. **Lord.** This can mean simply "sir," a polite form of address. Whereas in verse 21 it may have that intent, in this verse the author is using it in its sense as a title for deity since the rest of Martha's statement is full of spiritual insight into his identity. **the Messiah, the Son of God, who was to come into the world.** In calling him the Christ, Martha acknowledges Jesus as the One who delivers and saves his people from the power of sin and death. Her recognition of him as the Son of God shows her insight into his divine identity. The meaning behind this title is that he is God, sharing the Father's essential nature just as a child shares the characteristics of his or her parents. It was this claim to be the Son of God that was the real grounds for the opposition against him (19:7). The final phrase, **who was to come into the world,** refers to the expectation that one day a leader like Moses would arise (Deut. 18:18). This too acknowledges his authority and divine commission.

11:38 the tomb. Tombs for people of importance were either vertical shafts covered by a stone, or horizontal hollows carved out of a hill. Since this tomb is carved out of a cave, it would be the latter type.

11:40 Didn't I tell you. This may be a reference to the message in verse 4, or the implication of what he meant by his declaration to Martha in verse 25. The signs in the Gospel of John have consistently been regarded as demonstrations of Jesus' identity. They reveal his glory (2:11) and, based on them, people make decisions about who he is (6:14; 9:32–33). This final sign will reveal what has been alluded to all along—Jesus is God.

11:44 with linen strips and with his face wrapped in a cloth. While burial customs included wrapping the body with cloth and spices (19:40), this was not intended to preserve the body, like the ancient Egyptian process of mummification, but only as a sign of honor for the deceased person.

SESSION 12 : THE WITHERED FIG TREE

SCRIPTURE MARK 11:12—26

In last week's session, we saw Jesus' resurrection power as he raised his friend Lazarus from the dead. We were reminded that Jesus has conquered death and eternal life awaits those who belong to him. This week we will look at a miracle that Jesus did involving a fig tree, and we will consider what this act says to us about the need for our lives to be fruitful.

ICE-BREAKER : CONNECT WITH YOUR GROUP | 15 MINUTES

LEADER: Open with a word of prayer, and then have your group discuss one, two or all three of the Ice-Breaker questions.

Sometimes Christians are taught that it is wrong to get angry, but in our story for today we will see Jesus getting quite angry over some things that happened in the temple. Take turns sharing something about your own "anger history."

1. When you were a child, what were you taught about expressing anger?
   - ❑ "Good children don't."
   - ❑ "We don't get mad—we get even!"
   - ❑ "He who shouts the loudest wins."
   - ❑ "First, count to ten ... "
   - ❑ "Never go to bed angry."
   - ❑ Other _____.

2. When you were in high school, what do you remember getting the angriest about?
   - ❑ "Unfair" parental restrictions.
   - ❑ Favoritism toward a sibling.
   - ❑ My own failures.
   - ❑ Social injustice.
   - ❑ Friends who "stabbed me in the back."
   - ❑ Other _____.

3. What injustice gets you the angriest today?

LEADER: Select a member of the group ahead of time to read aloud the Scripture passage. Then discuss the Questions for Interaction, dividing into subgroups of three to six.

The following passage actually contains two stories: the cursing of a fig tree that then withers, and the "cleansing of the temple." The cursing of the fig is the only recorded miracle of Jesus where something is destroyed, and the "cleansing of the temple" helps us see why he performed it–it was a symbolic act of judgment against Israel. Read Mark 11:12-26, and note how Jesus explains the purpose of the withered fig tree.

The Withered Fig Tree

[12]The next day, when they came out from Bethany, He was hungry. [13]After seeing in the distance a fig tree with leaves, He went to find out if there was anything on it. When He came to it, He found nothing but leaves, because it was not the season for figs. [14]And He said to it, "May no one ever eat fruit from you again!" And His disciples heard it.

[15]They came to Jerusalem, and He went into the temple complex and began to throw out those buying and selling in the temple. He overturned the money changers' tables and the chairs of those selling doves, [16]and would not permit anyone to carry goods through the temple complex.

[17]Then He began to teach them: "Is it not written, 'My house will be called a house of prayer for all nations'? But you have made it 'a den of thieves!' " [18]Then the chief priests and the scribes heard it and started looking for a way to destroy Him. For they were afraid of Him, because the whole crowd was astonished by His teaching.

[19]And whenever evening came, they would go out of the city.

[20]Early in the morning, as they were passing by, they saw the fig tree withered from the roots up. [21]Then Peter remembered and said to Him, "Rabbi, look! The fig tree that You cursed is withered."

[22]Jesus replied to them, "Have faith in God. [23]I assure you: If anyone says to this mountain, 'Be lifted up and thrown into the sea,' and does not doubt in his heart, but believes that what he says will happen, it will be done for him. [24]Therefore, I tell you, all the things you pray and ask for–believe that you have received them, and you will have them. [25]And whenever you stand praying, if you have anything against anyone, forgive him, so that your Father in heaven may also forgive you your wrongdoing. [26]But if you don't forgive, neither will your Father in heaven forgive your wrongdoing."

Mark 11:12-26

LEADER: Refer to the Summary and Study Notes at the end of this section as needed. If 30 minutes is not enough time to answer all of the questions in this section, conclude the Bible Study by answering questions 6 and 7.

1. What is your initial response to this passage? What do you learn about Jesus from this story?

2. Given what you know about the religious leaders at the time of Jesus, what parallels do you see between them and the fig tree in verse 13? In what ways did they cover their fruitlessness with flashy foliage?

3. Why does Jesus get so angry at the people in the temple? What does this story say to us about the expression of anger?

4. How does the miracle of the withered fig tree serve as a springboard to Jesus' teaching about faith and prayer?

5. What conditions for effective prayer are raised in verses 22–26?

6. Compared to a fig tree, where are you these days spiritually?
   - ❏ A new shoot—I'm just starting out and there's not much to judge yet!
   - ❏ In full leaf—the foliage looks good, but there's no real fruit being produced.
   - ❏ Bearing fruit—my faith is having visible results in my serving God and others.
   - ❏ Picked clean—I was "bearing fruit" at one time, but everyone has used it all up!
   - ❏ Other _____.

7. What would have to change in order for you to be more fruitful?
   - ❏ I need to let God nurture my growth.
   - ❏ I need to be pruned to get rid of unproductive branches that are draining me.
   - ❏ I need to be transplanted into a more supportive environment.
   - ❏ I need to quit being concerned about the "foliage" and start producing fruit.
   - ❏ Other _____.

8. Were Jesus to walk into a church today, what might tempt him to once again take a whip to those abusing his "house of prayer"? What should we be doing to "cleanse" the church?

CARING TIME : APPLY THE LESSON AND PRAY FOR ONE ANOTHER | 15 MIN.

LEADER: Following the Caring Time, discuss with your group how they would like to celebrate the last session next week. Also, discuss the possibility of splitting into two groups and continuing with another study.

Come together now and encourage one another with the hope that Jesus has given us through his words about prayer in today's Scripture (especially v. 24). Begin by sharing your responses to the following questions. Then share prayer requests and close in a group prayer.

1. What have you dreamed about doing for God, but felt that it was just not possible?

2. How can this group be in prayer about the injustices of the world (see question 3 in the Ice-breaker section)?

3. What can this group do to help you be more fruitful in your spiritual life?

NEXT WEEK

Today we considered the only miracle Jesus ever did where something was destroyed—the cursing of a fig tree that made it wither. We examined what this means and how we need to have more faith and be fruitful. In the coming week, be in prayer about your answer to the Caring Time question 1, and consider how God might want you to reach out in faith to accomplish something for the kingdom. Next week we will look at the miraculous amount of fish that Jesus helped the disciples catch after his resurrection. We will give some thought to what this means for our own commission to share the Gospel.

Summary: The cursing and the withering of the fig tree is the only incident of a miracle of Jesus that is destructive in nature. Between the curse (v. 14) and its withering (v. 20), Mark sandwiches the story of the cleansing of the temple. Each story helps interpret the other. Both illustrate the judgment that is coming on Jerusalem. The disciples' surprise upon discovering the withered fig tree leads to a discussion about faith and prayer.

11:13 fig tree. On the Mount of Olives fig trees are in leaf by early April, but they would not have ripe fruit until June, long after the Passover. Fig trees were a common prophetic symbol associated with Israel and with judgment (Jer. 8:13; Hos. 9:10; Mic. 7:1).

11:14 His disciples heard it. Jesus has done something so seemingly out of character (cursing a fig tree for not doing what it could not do) that the disciples cannot help but notice. Since there is no obvious reason for his action (Mark has taken care to point out that "it was not the season for figs"), they are forced to ponder why he did this. This, of course, was his intention. In the same way that he often used extravagant language to make his point (9:42–43), here Jesus uses extravagant actions to get across this crucial point. Such acted-out parables were very much a part of how the Old Testament prophets communicated (Isa. 20; Ezek. 4–5).

11:15 buying and selling. The system of worship in the temple was built around sacrifice. The actual act of selling the animals in the temple area was not in itself a problem since this had originally been instituted as a means of assisting Jewish pilgrims who had to travel long distances to come to Jerusalem. Since they could obtain an animal for sacrifice at the temple, they would not have to deal with the problems of having a lamb traveling with them. However, by this time what once was a helpful service had become a racket. People could only offer an unblemished animal as a sacrifice, and the animal had to be inspected first. Apparently, the temple inspectors approved only those animals bought from certified vendors who sold the animals at a huge markup. These merchants actually worked for members of the high priest's family. As a result, the priests, the merchants and the inspectors all made a profit by taking advantage of the religious obligations of the Jewish people. **money changers' tables.** At Passover each Jew was required to pay a temple tax of one-half shekel (nearly two days' wages). No other currency was acceptable, necessitating money changers to exchange the money of pilgrims coming from outside Jerusalem. The money changers, however, charged exorbitant amounts for the simple act of exchanging currency: up to one-half day's wages of working people. **those selling doves.** Temple vendors charged 20 times what it cost to buy a dove outside the temple.

11:17 a house of prayer for all nations. This is a quote from Isaiah 56:7. Isaiah had a vision of the temple as a gathering place where all types of people might gather in common, reverent, joyful worship of God. The outermost area of the temple where all these activities were taking place was called the Court of the Gentiles since it was the only part of the temple Gentiles could enter (the other sections of the temple were reserved only for Jews). Instead of pursuing Isaiah's vision, the temple authorities had allowed this court to be turned into a raucous oriental bazaar, making prayer impossible. **den of thieves.** This is a quote from Jeremiah 7:11 where God rebukes the religious authorities of that day for using religion as a cloak for injustice.

11:18 The chief priests were Sadducees, and the scribes were typically Pharisees. The two sects normally did not cooperate together since they had so many differences between them, but they acted as one in their decision regarding Jesus. Rather than responding with repentance, the religious leaders plotted how to kill Jesus. Their concern was that the people might listen to him, resist their leadership and revolt against their system.

11:19 they would go out of the city. Pilgrims coming to Jerusalem for Passover would often stay outside the city at night. In Jesus' case, this probably also served a protective purpose, since that way those seeking to do him harm would have more difficulty locating him at night when the crowds would not be around him.

11:20 withered from the roots up. In light of the cleansing of the temple, the meaning of the withered fig tree becomes clear. This is what will happen to Israel. Judgment is coming to Jerusalem and on the temple in particular. The fig tree's fate will be the temple's fate. The temple was, in fact, destroyed by the Romans in A.D. 70 after a violent Jewish revolt against the empire. It has never been rebuilt.

11:23 this mountain ... into the sea. This is probably the Mount of Olives overlooking Jerusalem. The Dead Sea is visible from the Mount of Olives. Interestingly, Revelation speaks of a mountain indeed thrown into the heart of the sea (Rev. 8:8.) There it seems to represent the destruction of a fallen angel or other enemy of God. This may then refer not simply to prayer giving us random magical power, but the power to fight with God against the enemies of God.

11:25 See also Matthew 6:12–14. These types of commands are not meant to encourage a sense of bargaining with God, as if the disciple is to wring forgiveness out of God by making sure he or she is not holding a grudge against anyone else. Such commands simply are a reflection that the recognition of our great debt before God is what moves us to freely forgive those who have sinned against us.

SESSION 13 : THE CATCH OF FISH

SCRIPTURE JOHN 21:1–14

LAST WEEK

Jesus reminded us in last week's Scripture passage to "Have faith in God" (Mark 11:22), as he demonstrated his power by causing a fig tree to wither. We were also reminded by this miracle and the cleansing of the temple to bear fruit in our lives and to get rid of unproductive "branches." This week, in our final session, we will look at the miraculous catch of fish that Jesus enabled after his resurrection. More importantly, we will explore what this catch of fish means to us as we go out to spread the Gospel to the world.

ICE-BREAKER : CONNECT WITH YOUR GROUP | 15 MINUTES

LEADER: Begin this final session with a word of prayer and thanksgiving for this time together. Choose one or two Ice-Breaker questions to discuss.

Does anyone have some "fish stories" to tell? Now is your chance. Our Scripture today is a miraculous fish story, which even includes eating them around the campfire. Take turns sharing your own stories about fishing and campfires.

1. What is the best memory you have related to fishing? What made the experience special to you?

2. If you could rate your fishing proficiency from 1 ("I catch 'em in the frozen food section") to 10 ("I could have landed Moby Dick"), how would you rate yourself?

3. What is your favorite food to eat around a campfire?

LEADER: Select a member of the group ahead of time to read aloud the Scripture passage. Then discuss the Questions for Interaction, dividing into subgroups of three to six. Be sure to save some extra time at the end for the Caring Time.

Jesus was not a fisherman, so in the following story his disciples (who were fishermen by trade) could have very easily decided to ignore his advice. But one thing they had learned while following Jesus was that if he said something, they had better pay attention. Their obedience to this command brought dramatic results. Read John 21:1–14, and note how Jesus serves the disciples once again.

Jesus and the Miraculous Catch of Fish

21 After this, Jesus revealed Himself again to His disciples by the Sea of Tiberias. He revealed Himself in this way:

²Simon Peter, Thomas (called "Twin"), Nathanael from Cana of Galilee, Zebedee's sons, and two others of His disciples were together.

³"I'm going fishing," Simon Peter said to them.

"We're coming with you," they told him. They went out and got into the boat; but that night they caught nothing.

⁴When daybreak came, Jesus stood on the shore. However, the disciples did not know that it was Jesus.

⁵"Men," Jesus called to them, "you don't have any fish, do you?"

"No," they answered.

⁶"Cast the net on the right side of the boat," He told them, "and you'll find some." So they did, and they were unable to haul it in because of the large number of fish. ⁷Therefore the disciple whom Jesus loved said to Peter, "It's the Lord!"

When Simon Peter heard that it was the Lord, he tied his outer garment around him (for he was stripped) and plunged into the sea. ⁸But since they were not far from land (about 100 yards away), the other disciples came in the boat, dragging the net full of fish. ⁹When they got out on land, they saw a charcoal fire there, with fish lying on it, and bread.

¹⁰"Bring some of the fish you've just caught," Jesus told them. ¹¹So Simon Peter got up and hauled the net ashore, full of large fish–153 of them. Even though there were so many, the net was not torn.

¹²"Come and have breakfast," Jesus told them. None of the disciples dared ask Him, "Who are You?" because they knew it was the Lord. ¹³Jesus came, took the bread, and gave it to them. He did the same with the fish.

¹⁴This was now the third time Jesus appeared to the disciples after He was raised from the dead.

John 21:1–14

QUESTIONS FOR INTERACTION

LEADER: Refer to the Summary and Study Notes at the end of this section as needed. If 30 minutes is not enough time to answer all of the questions in this section, conclude the Bible Study by answering question 7.

1. Why do you think Peter and the other disciples went back to Peter's home territory of Galilee?
   - ☐ To relax and do some fishing.
   - ☐ To go back to their old occupation.
   - ☐ To put their lives back together.
   - ☐ To forget about Jesus.
   - ☐ To obey Jesus' instructions to go to Galilee and wait for him there.
   - ☐ Other _____.

2. Why did Jesus' followers have difficulty recognizing him?

3. How do you think the disciples felt when Jesus told them to throw their net on the right side of the boat? Why do you think they obeyed?

4. Why did Peter jump out of the boat and wade ashore instead of staying with the others and helping them haul the fish ashore?
   - ☐ He was too energized to wait.
   - ☐ He was too full of guilt to wait.
   - ☐ He was eager to see Jesus close up.
   - ☐ He was the boss and he could do what he wanted.
   - ☐ He was so eager to see his Lord that he could not wait.
   - ☐ Other _____.

5. What do you see as Jesus' purpose in providing a miraculous catch of fish and then making breakfast for these disciples?

6. If you were Peter and knew you had just recently "blown it" by denying Jesus, how would you be feeling about the miraculous catch of fish and the breakfast Jesus served?

7. When it comes to understanding Jesus' call upon your life now, are you still "fishing in the dark" (v. 3) or meeting with him in the light of dawn (vv. 12–13)? Why do you answer as you do? What is the next step for you?

If your group has time and/or wants a challenge, go on to this question.

8. What connection do you see between this story and the Lord's Supper?

CARING TIME : APPLY THE LESSON AND PRAY FOR ONE ANOTHER | 15 MIN.

LEADER: Conclude this final Caring Time by praying for each group member and asking for God's blessing in any plans to start a new group or continue to study together.

Gather around each other now in this final time of sharing and prayer and encourage one another to have faith and hope as you go out into the world.

1. What was your serendipity (unexpected blessing) during this course?

2. Where is Christ calling you right now to "throw your nets" to live a more productive life for him? What help do you need to find this direction?

3. Where do you need a second chance in your life, like the one Peter received? How can this group continue to pray for you in the weeks ahead?

Summary: Right at the beginning of his ministry Jesus told his disciples, "I will make you fishers of men!" (Matt. 4:19). And now here at the end of his earthly ministry, after his resurrection, Jesus performed this miracle to show his disciples how much power he would give them to help them in their performance of this task. It was not that Jesus thought they actually needed all the fish they caught that day. What they needed most of all was the knowledge and confidence that when they went out to "fish" for people in his name, there would be no limitation to what they could do if they were just obedient to his word.

21:1 Sea of Tiberias. Tiberias was a city founded on the shore of the Sea of Galilee in 20 A.D. by Herod. By the time the Gospel of John was written, this new name for the Sea of Galilee had become well known.

21:2 On this occasion seven of the disciples are together. Five are identified. The Sons of Zebedee are James and John (Mark 1:19–20). The two anonymous disciples may be unnamed because they have not previously been featured in the gospel of John. Nathanael was mentioned as one of the earliest followers of Jesus (1:44–51), but his name does not appear in any list of the Twelve (Mark 3:16–19). A common guess is that he is the Bartholomew whose name does appear.

21:3 I'm going fishing. It is certainly not surprising that as these disciples wait for the Lord in Galilee (as they have been instructed) they should decide to go fishing, as this was their original trade (Mark 1:16–20). But, in fact, this action on their part has another, metaphoric, dimension. When Jesus called these four men to follow him he promised them he would make them "fishers of men" (Mark 1:17). On their own, the disciples are not going to become this sort of fishermen. They have labored all night and come up empty. But then Jesus comes and instructs them how to fish (v. 6), and they become successful. This is a vivid prediction of what is ahead for the disciples. They will be empowered by Jesus to become successful fishers of people.

21:4 did not know that it was Jesus. Mary Magdalene had the same difficulty (20:14). Paul writes of the resurrection body being different than the physical body (1 Cor. 15:35–44), and this may explain why such difficulties happened.

21:6 Cast the net on the right side. Luke reports Jesus giving similar fishing advice to Peter and the others at the time he first called them (Luke 5:1–11).

21:7 the disciple whom Jesus loved. This is thought to be John, the author of this gospel. **It's the Lord!** As Jesus' voice opened Mary's eyes to recognize him (20:16), so here the enormous catch of fish revealed to the beloved disciple that the one with whom they were talking was the Lord.

21:9 they saw a charcoal fire there. It is interesting that the same word used in 18:18 to describe the fire around which Peter was standing when he betrayed Jesus, is used here to describe the fire at which Jesus will draw Peter back into the company of his disciples (21:15–17). These are the only two uses of this term in the New Testament.

21:11 153. Jerome reported that at the time it was thought that there were 153 species of fish. If this is meant as an allusion to this, it may have been intended to symbolize people of every color. and culture, caught in the net of the kingdom and not lost ("the net was not torn").

21:12 breakfast. The Jesus that they met was no disembodied spirit. They could see him and hear him and eat with him. He had hands and feet that allowed him to kindle a fire on the beach. Jesus had been resurrected bodily. He had conquered death.

21:13 Jesus came, took the bread, and gave it to them. In the gospel of John there is no account of the Last Supper. However, the words used here are very similar to words used at the Last Supper (Mark 14:22). Furthermore, the bread and the fish are reminiscent of the feeding of the five thousand, where there is a clear parallel to Communion. It is through participation in this meal that the disciples come to recognize who Jesus is. A similar thing happens in Luke 24:30-31. The disciples on the road to Emmaus meet a mysterious stranger whom they discover—in the breaking of the bread—to be Jesus.

21:14 the third time. This is the third appearing of Jesus to his disciples. described in John's gospel (20:19-23,24-29). The post-resurrection appearances are important for a number of reasons. For one thing, they are part of the proof of Jesus' resurrection (along with the fact of the empty tomb, the collapsed and empty grave clothes, etc.) Second, they show that Jesus had conquered death. He was not simply a disembodied spirit who appeared as a ghost-like figure, a hallucination or a vision. Third, they describe how it was that the disciples learned of their mission. Fourth, it was the encounter with the living Jesus that changed the disciples from frightened men in hiding to bold witnesses who changed the world. Finally, the post-resurrection appearances show to all of us that Jesus is still alive and thus we can enter into a personal relationship with him even today.

Personal Notes

Personal Notes

_____

_____

_____

_____

_____

_____

_____

_____

_____

_____

_____

_____

Personal Notes

Personal Notes

PERSONAL NOTES

_____

_____

_____

_____

_____

_____

_____

_____

_____

_____

_____

_____

PERSONAL NOTES

_____

_____

_____

_____

_____

_____

_____

_____

_____

_____

_____

_____

Personal notes

_____

_____

_____

_____

_____

_____

_____

_____

_____

_____

_____

_____

Personal Notes